Forceful Persuasion

Forceful Persuasion
Coercive Diplomacy as an Alternative to War

Alexander L. George

Foreword by Ambassador Samuel W. Lewis

UNITED STATES
INSTITUTE OF PEACE PRESS

Washington, D.C.

The views expressed in this book are those of the author alone. They do not necessarily reflect views of the United States Institute of Peace.

United States Institute of Peace
1550 M Street, N.W.
Washington, D.C. 20005

Second printing 1993

Printed in the United States of America

Library of Congress Cataloging-in-Publication Data
George, Alexander L.
    Forceful persuasion : coercive diplomacy as an alternative to war / Alexander L. George ; foreword by Samuel W. Lewis.
        p.   cm.
    Includes bibliographical references and index.
    ISBN 1-878379-14-3
    1. United States—Foreign relations—1945- 2. Diplomacy.
3. Aggression (International law) 4. International relations.
5. Ultimatums.   6. Sanctions (International law) I. Title.
JX1417.G445   1992
327.2—dc20   91-44803
                                                    CIP

United States Institute of Peace

The United States Institute of Peace is an independent, nonpartisan, federal institution created and funded by Congress to strengthen the nation's capacity to promote the peaceful resolution of international conflict. Established in 1984, the Institute has its origins in the tradition of American statesmanship, which seeks to limit international violence and to achieve a just peace based on freedom and human dignity. The Institute meets its congressional mandate to expand available knowledge about ways to achieve a more peaceful world through an array of programs including grantmaking, a three-tiered fellowship program, research and studies projects, development of library resources, and a variety of citizen education activities. The Institute is governed by a bipartisan, fifteen-member Board of Directors, including four members ex officio from the executive branch of the federal government and eleven individuals appointed from outside federal service by the President of the United States and confirmed by the Senate.

Contents

Foreword *by Samuel W. Lewis*   ix

Preface   xi

Part One *The General Theory and Logic of
Coercive Diplomacy*   3

The Concept of Coercive Diplomacy   4

Variants of Coercive Diplomacy Strategy   7

Two Levels of Communication in Coercive Diplomacy   9

The Carrot-and-Stick Approach   10

The Central Task of Coercive Diplomacy   11

Part Two *The Practice of Coercive Diplomacy:
Case Studies*   15

1. United States–Japan Relations Leading to Pearl
   Harbor: Coercive Diplomacy That Boomeranged   19

2. The Laos Crisis of 1961–62: Coercive Diplomacy for
   Minimal Objectives   25

3. The Cuban Missile Crisis: Peaceful Resolution
   Through Coercive Diplomacy   31

4. Vietnam 1965: The Failure of Air Power to
   Coerce Hanoi   39

5. The Reagan Administration's Use of Coercive
   Diplomacy Against Nicaragua   47

6. U.S. Coercive Diplomacy Against Libyan-Inspired
   Terrorism, December 1985–April 1986   53

7. The Persian Gulf Crisis: A Tough Case for Coercive
   Diplomacy   59

Part Three   *Findings and Conclusions*   67

Flexibility of the Strategy of Coercive Diplomacy   67

Contextual Variables Affecting Coercive Diplomacy   69

The Constraints and Risks of Ultimatums   72

Components of Crisis Bargaining: Persuasion,
Coercion, Accommodation   73

Conditions That Favor Coercive Diplomacy   75

Conclusions   82

Notes   85

Bibliographical Notes and Acknowledgments   89

Index   93

Foreword

When Iraq invaded Kuwait in August 1990, most of the world condemned the invasion but few nations recommended immediate military action to redress the situation. Instead, the major powers, acting through the United Nations, concluded that the best approach would be to pursue a policy that combined diplomatic efforts with the threat of force. Accordingly, the UN Security Council passed several resolutions that first imposed economic sanctions and then authorized the use of military force to roll back the Iraqi aggression.

Such a policy, called coercive diplomacy by eminent political scientist Alexander George, refers to a defensive strategy that attempts to persuade an opponent to stop or undo an aggressive action. This strategy involves the threat of force or a limited exemplary use of force as a means of restoring peace in a diplomatic crisis. The hope is that these measures will lead to a diplomatic solution that will save lives in the long run by avoiding a much greater use of force later.

In the case of the Gulf crisis, unfortunately, coercive diplomacy did not succeed; Saddam Hussein did not withdraw from Kuwait and the U.S.-led coalition eventually decided to launch a full-scale war against Iraqi forces. But coercive diplomacy has had its successes, most notably during the Cuban missile crisis of 1962. And it continues to be an alluring strategy for policymakers because it offers the possibility of avoiding war (if it is successful).

In discussing coercive diplomacy, George distinguishes it from both blackmail—the use of threats to persuade an opponent to give up something without resistance—and deterrence—the use of threats to dissuade an opponent from taking an action not yet initiated. And the efficacy of coercive diplomacy can be enhanced by offering positive inducements along with punitive threats, as President Kennedy did towards the end of the Cuban missile crisis by secretly offering to remove Jupiter missiles from Turkey.

In this cogent analysis, George first briefly describes the theory of coercive diplomacy and then examines seven examples of U.S. diplomacy that span the globe. In addition to the cases mentioned above, he discusses the oil embargo imposed on Japan just before Pearl Harbor, the threats of military intervention during the Laos crisis of 1961–62, the use of limited air strikes against North Vietnam in 1965, efforts to undermine the Sandinista government in the 1980s, and the April 1986 air attack on Libya. He concludes by analyzing the usefulness and limitations of coercive diplomacy.

It should be emphasized that coercive diplomacy is only one of several tools that nations can employ in seeking to restrain or resolve international conflict. It works well in some situations; in others it is ineffective or inappropriate. *Forceful Persuasion* should better enable us to distinguish the former situations from the latter.

Samuel W. Lewis, President
United States Institute of Peace

Preface

Coercive diplomacy, as it is defined in this study, is a strategy that is sometimes employed by policymakers in the hope of securing a peaceful resolution of a serious dispute. Because some readers may regard "coercive diplomacy" as an infelicitous and unfortunate term, it may be useful to explain that it is employed here because it does convey that threats are sometimes employed as an instrument of peaceful diplomacy and that the strategy of coercive diplomacy offers an alternative to reliance on military strategy in a dispute with other states. It may strike some readers as incongruous that coercion could contribute to maintaining or restoring peace in a diplomatic crisis. But it must be recognized that sometimes threats can be combined with diplomatic efforts to persuade an opponent to stop or undo his effort to alter a status quo situation that itself endangers the peace or, as in the case of the recent Persian Gulf crisis, already involves naked military aggression.

The response of the United States and the Security Council to Iraq's invasion of Kuwait has aroused new interest in coercive persuasion as a possible way of achieving diplomatic objectives without having to resort to war. The employment of economic sanctions against Iraq, strongly reinforced in

November 1990 by a threat to engage in military action if
necessary, qualifies as an example of the strategy of coercive
diplomacy. In the end, coercive diplomacy failed and war followed. The possibility that the strategy of coercive diplomacy
could provide a peaceful alternative to war was stretched to
the limit in the Gulf crisis. A better understanding of why
this was so can be gained by viewing the effort to employ
coercive diplomacy in the Gulf crisis from the perspective of
the analytical framework provided in this monograph and by
comparing the Gulf crisis with previous crises in which the
strategy of coercive diplomacy was employed.

My interest in studying coercive diplomacy precedes the
Persian Gulf crisis by twenty-five years. It was aroused in the
early spring of 1965 when I was asked by the president of
the RAND Corporation, Frank Collbohm, to comment on a
thesis advanced by an Air Force general which held that U.S.
air power had not succeeded in intimidating North Vietnam's
leaders in March-April of that year because it had not been
properly employed. In this connection the general objected
to the limited use of air power as part of a weak strategy of
graduated escalation, but, it seemed to me, he conveyed no
understanding or appreciation of the political and diplomatic constraints that had led President Johnson to rule out
bolder use of air power in a stronger variant of coercive diplomacy. The general's thesis appeared dubious to me also
because I sensed that conditions for a stronger, possibly effective type of coercive persuasion had not existed in this
case. To test my hunch I compared the effort to use limited
U.S. air attacks against North Vietnam as a means of trying
to persuade its leaders to accept the demand that they cease
support for the Viet Minh in South Vietnam with President
Kennedy's successful use of threats of force in 1962 to persuade Nikita Khrushchev to remove his missiles from Cuba.
Comparing the two cases helped me to identify a number of
conditions present in the Cuban missile case that seemed to
have contributed to successful coercion on that occasion. The

absence of the same conditions in the Vietnam 1965 case seemed to be part of the explanation for the failure of coercive persuasion on that occasion. However, the conclusions I drew from the comparison of the two cases were highly provisional, because both the conceptualization of coercive diplomacy and the methodology that I employed were rudimentary.[1]

While at RAND I became interested in improving methodology for studies of this kind. The task was a challenging one: How can one study past crises in order to draw useful lessons? And how can one aggregate and cumulate the findings of such case studies into a form of policy-relevant theory, or what some prefer to call "generic knowledge," about the uses and limitations of strategies such as deterrence and crisis management as well as coercive diplomacy? Over a period of years I eventually developed a set of methodological procedures for this purpose that I call the "method of structured, focused comparison."[2] (I mention this here because I have employed a version of this method in the present study.) To this end in 1966, while still at RAND, I initiated a research program, "Bridging the Gap between Theory and Practice in Foreign Policy." I continued and expanded this program of studies after I joined the faculty at Stanford University in 1968.

At Stanford I soon undertook, with two collaborators, a somewhat more systematic study of coercive diplomacy, this time elaborating a fuller, more satisfactory conceptualization of the abstract theory of coercive diplomacy. We studied the Cuban missile crisis and Vietnam cases in much more detail than in my initial effort at RAND, and we added a third case on President Kennedy's use of coercive persuasion in the Laos crisis of 1961–62.[3] It would have been desirable, but was not possible on that occasion, to have included additional historical cases in which coercive diplomacy was attempted. Still, comparing two cases in which the strategy succeeded (Laos and Cuba) with one case in which it did not (Vietnam

1965) gave us a good start in identifying various conditions which, if present in a particular case, favored successful persuasion and which, if absent, contributed to its failure. Also, the marked differences among the three cases enabled us to identify several different variants of the strategy of coercive diplomacy (the "try-and-see" and the "ultimatum") and to identify various constraints on the choice and implementation of a particular form of the strategy.

Finally, and perhaps most important, this early study enabled us to see the need to make a sharper distinction between an abstract theory and various strategies of coercive diplomacy, a distinction that is more fully developed in the present study. The 1971 study emphasized particularly the difficult task that policymakers face in trying to formulate a strategy of coercive diplomacy that fits the peculiar configuration of each situation in which it is to be employed. In discussing this task of "operationalizing" the general model of coercive diplomacy we called attention to some of the risks and uncertainties of the strategy.

Since it was published in 1971, this treatment of coercive diplomacy has withstood reasonably well the test of time and the critical scrutiny of other investigators, some of whom have drawn upon it, and others who have made helpful suggestions for improving the understanding of strategies of coercive persuasion. For some years, however, I have felt the need to update the 1971 study and increase the number of historical cases included. A brief update of the earlier study is offered in this slender volume because, as the recent Persian Gulf crisis indicates, interest in the uses and limitations of the strategy of coercive diplomacy is by no means confined to academic specialists but can at any time unexpectedly become a preoccupation and priority for policymakers. A study of the failure of coercive diplomacy against Saddam Hussein is included in this volume and can be better understood, I believe, by the comparison provided with other cases in which that strategy was successful.

Although the present study builds to a considerable extent on the 1971 volume, the inclusion of four additional cases and the opportunity to reconsider, refine, and elaborate both the abstract model of coercive diplomacy and generic knowledge regarding conditions affecting the efficacy of this strategy should make it more useful both for scholars and policymakers than the 1971 study. In the present study a much sharper distinction is drawn between abstract theory and generic knowledge. Additional variants of the strategy are identified and a richer body of generic knowledge is provided.

Finally, several caveats must be stated. First, generic knowledge of coercive diplomacy remains provisional and incomplete. It will and should continue to be refined with the study of additional historical cases and further reconsideration of the seven included in the present study. Second, to study coercive diplomacy and to refine knowledge of it is not to advocate its use. As will be seen, this strategy is highly context-dependent; not only are many variables imbedded in any particular situation that influence the results, but policymakers can expect to encounter important uncertainties and risks in attempting to use it. It is hoped that this study will assist policy analysts to make a more discriminating and accurate diagnosis of situations in which coercive diplomacy might be employed so that they can judge whether it is likely to be a viable option in a particular situation. It must be recognized that coercive diplomacy is a beguiling strategy insofar as it offers an attractive possibility for achieving one's objective without having to rely on force. However, the very act of engaging in coercive diplomacy strengthens one's commitment on behalf of the objective, engages further one's reputation and prestige, and makes it difficult not to take additional action if the effort to intimidate the opponent fails.

Forceful Persuasion

part one

The General Theory and Logic of Coercive Diplomacy

In this part of the study I describe in some detail the *general, abstract theory* of coercive diplomacy which, properly understood, should be useful both to policymakers and scholars.

I emphasize that the abstract theory is not itself a strategy of coercive diplomacy. Rather, the abstract theory familiarizes policymakers with the general characteristics of coercive diplomacy and the logic on which its presumed efficacy rests. Therefore, it should be thought of as no more than an aid to enable policymakers to consider more carefully the possible use of a strategy of coercive diplomacy in a particular situation. Part One of this study also provides policymakers with an indication of different variants of the strategy and a starting point for judging whether they can design a strategy that fits the configuration of the situation at hand. What the abstract theory does *not* do is provide policymakers with a basis for judging whether coercive diplomacy is likely to be effective in a particular situation. Rather, policymakers must turn to *generic knowledge* derived from study of a variety of past cases to make such judgments.

3

The abstract theory should also be useful to scholars who study past cases of coercive diplomacy in order to develop generic knowledge of the conditions and processes associated with success or failure of a strategy. The generic knowledge that can be gained from the seven historical cases analyzed in Part Two of this monograph is presented in Part Three.

Coercive diplomacy, or coercive persuasion as some might prefer to call it, is not an esoteric concept. Intimidation of one kind or another in order to get others to comply with one's wishes is an everyday occurrence in human affairs. And what we refer to as coercive diplomacy has often been employed in the long history of international conflict, sometimes successfully and sometimes not. The general idea of coercive diplomacy is to back one's demand on an adversary with a threat of punishment for noncompliance that he will consider credible and potent enough to persuade him to comply with the demand. Hence, it should be noted, the abstract theory of coercive diplomacy assumes pure rationality on the part of the opponent—an ability to receive all relevant information, evaluate it correctly, make proper judgments as to the credibility and potency of the threat, and see that it is in his interest to accede to the demand made on him. The abstract theory of coercive diplomacy, therefore, does not take into account the possibility of misperception and miscalculation or that an opponent's "rationality" is affected by psychological variables and by values, culture, and tradition that may differ from those of the coercive state. These possibilities are of critical importance and must receive careful attention whenever policymakers attempt to devise a strategy of coercive diplomacy in a particular situation against a particular opponent.

The Concept of Coercive Diplomacy
First, we need to clarify how the concept of coercive diplomacy is being used in this study and to differentiate it from

other ways threats are used as an instrument of policy.[1] In this study the term coercive diplomacy is restricted to *defensive* uses of the strategy—that is, efforts to persuade an opponent to stop and/or undo an action he is already embarked upon. Of course coercive threats can also be employed aggressively to persuade a victim to give up something of value without putting up resistance. Such offensive uses of coercive threats are better designated by the term "blackmail strategy." Coercive diplomacy also needs to be distinguished from deterrence, a strategy that employs threats to dissuade an adversary from undertaking a damaging action in the future. In contrast, coercive diplomacy is a response to an encroachment already undertaken. The term "compellance," which Thomas Schelling introduced into the literature over twenty years ago, is often employed to encompass both coercive diplomacy and blackmail. I prefer not to use that term for two reasons. First, it is useful to distinguish, as compellance does not, between defensive and offensive uses of coercive threats. Second, the concept of compellance implies exclusive or heavy reliance on coercive threats to influence an adversary, whereas I wish to emphasize the possibility of a more flexible diplomacy that can employ noncoercive persuasion and accommodation as well as coercive threats.

Coercive diplomacy does indeed offer an alternative to reliance on military action. It seeks to *persuade* an opponent to cease his aggression rather than bludgeon him into stopping. In contrast to the blunt use of force to repel an adversary, coercive diplomacy emphasizes the use of threats to punish the adversary if he does not comply with what is demanded of him. If force is used in coercive diplomacy, it consists of an exemplary use of quite limited force to persuade the opponent to back down. By "exemplary" I mean the use of just enough force of an appropriate kind to demonstrate resolution to protect one's interests and to establish the credibility of one's determination to use more force if necessary.[2] Even a relatively small exemplary action (for example, President

Kennedy's order to U.S. "civilian advisers" in Laos in April 1961 to put on their uniforms) can have a disproportionately large coercive impact if it is coupled with a credible threat of additional action. The strategy of coercive diplomacy, however, does not require use of exemplary actions. The crisis may be satisfactorily resolved without an exemplary use of force; or the strategy of coercive diplomacy may be abandoned in favor of full-scale military operations without a preliminary use of exemplary force.

In employing coercive diplomacy, which may already include nonmilitary sanctions, one gives the adversary an opportunity to stop or back off before one resorts to military operations. Notice that either of two demands can be made on the adversary. He may be asked merely to *stop* what he is doing; or he may be asked to *undo* what he has done—that is, to reverse what he has managed to accomplish. The first type of demand generally asks less of the opponent and may be easier to accomplish in a particular situation than the second type. The use of threats (and of exemplary use of limited force) should be closely coordinated with appropriate communications to the opponent. Therefore, signaling, bargaining, and negotiating are important dimensions of coercive diplomacy, though their roles vary in different crises.

Coercive diplomacy is an attractive strategy insofar as it offers the possibility of achieving one's objective in a crisis economically, with little or no bloodshed, fewer political and psychological costs, and often with less risk of unwanted escalation than does traditional military strategy. But for this very reason coercive diplomacy can be a beguiling strategy. Particularly leaders of militarily powerful countries may be tempted sometimes to believe that they can, with little risk, intimidate weaker opponents to give up their gains and their objectives. But, of course, the militarily weaker side may be strongly motivated by what is at stake and refuse to back down, in effect calling the bluff of the coercing power. The latter must then decide whether to back off, accept a compromise settlement, or escalate to the use of military force to gain its objective. In addition, as the case studies will illustrate, a powerful country may encounter other constraints, risks, and uncertainties in attempting to make effective use of the strategy.

Variants of Coercive Diplomacy Strategy

The general concept of coercive diplomacy, I suggest, contains a number of "empty boxes" (i.e., variables) that policymakers must fill in when constructing a particular strategy of coercive diplomacy to apply in a specific situation. Policymakers must decide (1) what to demand of the opponent; (2) whether and how to create a sense of urgency for compliance with the demand; (3) whether and what kind of punishment to threaten for noncompliance; and (4) whether to rely solely on the threat of punishment or also to offer conditional inducements of a positive character to secure acceptance of the demand.

Depending on how policymakers deal with these four components of the general model, significantly different variants of the strategy are possible. Let us identify first those variants of the strategy that stem from differences in how the first three variables are formulated.

The starkest variant of the strategy includes all three ingredients of a full-fledged ultimatum. A classic ultimatum has three components: (1) a demand on the opponent; (2) a time limit or sense of urgency for compliance with the demand; and (3) a threat of punishment for noncompliance that is both credible to the opponent and sufficiently potent to impress upon him that compliance is preferable. An ultimatum, although the starkest variant of coercive diplomacy, is not necessarily the most effective. There are often reasons why an ultimatum may be inappropriate, infeasible, or even highly risky in a particular situation. (I shall return to this point in Part Three.)

When an explicit time limit is not set forth but a sense of

real urgency is conveyed by other means, one may refer to this variant of the strategy as a "tacit" ultimatum, which is not, for that reason, necessarily less potent. Similarly, when the threat of punishment is not specifically set forth but nonetheless is credibly conveyed by actions, one may refer to this variant also as a tacit ultimatum. Forgoing the delivery of an explicit ultimatum, a state may prefer to convey the gist of it by some combination of military preparation and stern warning.

Let us turn now to other variants of coercive diplomacy in which one of the three components of an ultimatum is diluted or absent. One variant is the "try-and-see" approach. In this version of the strategy, only the first element of an ultimatum—a clear demand—is conveyed; the coercing power does not announce a time limit or convey a strong sense of urgency for compliance. Instead, it takes one limited coercive threat or action and waits to see whether it will suffice to persuade the opponent before threatening or taking another step. There are several versions of the try-and-see approach, as will be evident in some of the case studies.

Somewhat stronger in coercive impact, although still falling well short of the ultimatum, is the variant that relies on a "gradual turning of the screw." It differs from the try-and-see approach in that a threat to step up pressure gradually is conveyed at the outset and is carried out incrementally. At the same time, the gradual turning of the screw differs from the ultimatum in that it lacks a sense of time urgency for compliance and relies on the threat of a gradual, incremental increase in coercive pressure rather than threatening large escalation to strong, decisive military action if the opponent does not comply. In practice, the analytical distinction between try-and-see and turning of the screw may be blurred if the policymaker wavers or behaves inconsistently.

Several observations about these variants of coercive diplomacy will be made later. When an ultimatum or tacit ultimatum is simply not appropriate or feasible, or may be considered premature or too risky, a try-and-see or turning of the screw approach may be judged to fit better the domestic political-diplomatic-military configuration of the conflict situation. It should be noted that, as happened in some of our historical cases, policymakers may shift from one variant of coercive diplomacy to another.

Thus far we have presented distinctions among four different forms that the strategy of coercive diplomacy may take: the ultimatum, tacit ultimatum, try-and-see, and gradual turning of the screw variants. While such distinctions are useful for some purposes, it would be misleading to assume that the form of the strategy alone determines the likelihood of success. Certainly from a formalistic standpoint the ultimatum is a stronger, or starker, variant than the try-and-see approach. But the coercive impact of any form of the strategy and whether it will be effective depends on other factors.

Two Levels of Communication in Coercive Diplomacy

It is important to recognize that coercive diplomacy often operates on two levels of communication: words and actions. In addition to what is said, significant nonverbal communication or signaling can occur via either military moves or political-diplomatic activities. Nonverbal communication often emerges from the structure and development of the situation. Coercive persuasion depends not merely or exclusively on whether all three components of a classic ultimatum are present in verbal messages to the opponent. The structure of the situation as it develops can enhance or weaken the impact of coercive threats. The actions taken or not taken during the crisis—for example, whether and what kind of military forces are deployed or alerted, whether the coercing power undertakes political and diplomatic preparations of the kind needed to carry out its threats of force—can reinforce verbal threats and make them more credible or can dilute and weaken the impact of even strong verbal threats.

Actions may reinforce strong words, or they may compensate for weak words when it is not possible or prudent to utter strong words. But, contrary to the conventional wisdom, actions do not always speak louder than words. However strong the actions, they may be perceived by the adversary as equivocal or as bluffs. Words, then, may be needed in some situations to clarify the meaning of the actions taken or to convey unalterable commitment and resolution. Similarly, of course, actions may be needed to avoid the possibility that threatening words may be dismissed as bluff.

We conclude, therefore, that the relationship between actions and words—the two levels of communication—is likely to be very important in employing the strategy of coercive diplomacy. But there is no single, simple way of stating what the relationship between words and actions must be to ensure the success of the strategy. Crises in which coercive diplomacy is employed are replete with opportunities for miscommunication and miscalculation. And this is another aspect of coercive diplomacy that can make it an elusive, problematical, and risky strategy.

The Carrot-and-Stick Approach

The reader will have noted that the discussion of variants of coercive diplomacy thus far has focused exclusively, and much too narrowly, on the use of threats of punishment. We turn now to the fourth "empty box" or variable-component of the theory of coercive diplomacy—one that requires the policymaker to decide whether to rely solely on the threat of punishment or also to offer positive inducements. As in diplomacy more generally, the strategy of coercive diplomacy can use positive inducements and assurances as well as punitive threats to influence an adversary; when it does so it is often referred to as a strategy of "carrots and sticks." This approach greatly enhances the flexibility and adaptability of the strategy and gives the negotiation and bargaining dimensions of coercive diplomacy even greater prominence.

The policymaker must decide whether to rely exclusively or largely on the threat of punishment (as the United States and the United Nations coalition did in the Persian Gulf crisis) or also offer conditional positive inducements (as Kennedy finally did toward the end of the Cuban missile crisis). The carrot in such a strategy can be any of a variety of things the target of coercion values. And the magnitude and significance of the carrot can range from a seemingly trivial concession of a face-saving character to substantial concessions that bring about a settlement of the crisis through a genuine, balanced quid pro quo.

Whether coercive diplomacy will work in a particular case may depend on whether it relies solely on negative sanctions or combines threats with positive inducements and assurances. This point is of considerable practical as well as theoretical significance. Recognition that coercive diplomacy in principle can use a carrot-and-stick approach leaves open the question whether in practice the policymaker employing the strategy is willing or able to offer a positive inducement and, if so, to decide what conditional offer and concessions to make.

Nonetheless, the essential point remains: what the threatened stick cannot achieve by itself, unless it is a very formidable one, may possibly be achieved by combining it with a carrot. It should be said, too, that just as threats of punishment must be credible to the opponent, so must the positive inducements and reassurances offered be credible.

The Central Task of Coercive Diplomacy

Let us turn now to the central task of a coercive strategy: to create in the opponent the expectation of costs of sufficient magnitude to erode his motivation to continue what he is doing. As already noted, success may depend on whether the initial coercive action or threat stands alone or is part of a broader credible threat to escalate pressure further if necessary.

How much of a threat, or combination of threat with positive inducement, is necessary to persuade an opponent to comply? The abstract, general theory of coercive diplomacy tells us that the answer depends very much on two variables: what one demands of the opponent and how strongly disinclined he is to comply with that demand. Of course, these two variables are not independent of each other, and the relationship between them must receive the careful attention of the side that is employing a strategy of coercive diplomacy. The critical point to remember is that the strength of the opponent's motivation not to comply is highly dependent on what is demanded of him. Thus, asking relatively little of the opponent makes it easier for him to permit himself to be coerced. Conversely, demanding a great deal will strengthen an opponent's resistance and make the task of coercing him more difficult. Demanding a great deal may mean not only requiring an opponent to give up the material gains he has or is about to achieve but also requiring him to pay the often-substantial psychological and political costs of compliance with the demand. Also critical, of course, is the adversary's perception of the costs to him, which may be significantly greater than what the coercing power believes it is demanding.

The general, abstract theory correctly emphasizes that what is demanded of the opponent and his motivation to resist are closely related. As will be seen in the case studies, the outcome of coercive diplomacy is extremely sensitive to the relative motivations of the two sides. Motivation, in turn, reflects the way they perceive the balance of interests engaged by the dispute. Motivation here refers to each side's conception of what is at stake in the dispute, the importance it attaches to the various interests engaged by the crisis, and what costs and risks it is willing to incur on behalf of these interests. The choice of the demand made on the opponent, therefore, is of considerable importance in shaping the relative motivation of the two sides. Not only does the demand influence the level of the other side's motivation, as already noted; the motivation of the coercing power will also vary depending on the nature and magnitude of the demand it makes on the opponent. In other words, there is often an important strategic dimension to the choice of the objective on behalf of which coercive diplomacy is employed. Quite simply, it affects the motivation of both sides and the balance of motivation between them.

According to the logic of the abstract model of coercive diplomacy, it is more likely to be successful if the objective selected—and the demand made—by the coercing power reflects only the most important of its interests. Such a choice is more likely to create an asymmetry of interests, and therefore an asymmetry of motivation, in its favor. Conversely, if the coercing power pursues ambitious objectives that do not reflect its vital or very important interests or makes demands that infringe on vital or very important interests of the adversary, the asymmetry of interests and the balance of motivation is likely to operate in favor of the adversary. (The importance of asymmetry of motivation will be seen in several of the historical cases. For example, in the Cuban missile crisis President Kennedy limited his demand to removal of the missiles, an objective which he then succeeded in persuading Khrushchev was more important to the United States than it was to the Soviet Union. Had Kennedy chosen more ambitious objectives, as some of his advisers urged—the elimination of Castro or the removal of Soviet influence from Cuba—Khrushchev's motivation to resist would have been greater, and quite possibly the variable of relative motivation would have operated in his favor. That is, confronted by such demands, Khrushchev might have been willing to accept greater risks to prevent Kennedy from achieving those objectives than Kennedy would have been willing to accept to achieve them.)

The general theory emphasizes still another dimension of this central task of coercive diplomacy. It is not enough that the policymaker feel confident that he has conveyed a threat of punishment for noncompliance with his demand that is potent and credible enough to convince the opponent to comply. Rather, it is the *target's* estimate of the credibility and potency of the threat that is critical. As in so much of coercive diplomacy, many of the critical variables are psychological ones having to do with the perceptions and judgment of the target. The possibility of misperceptions and miscalculations by the opponent is ever present and can determine the outcome.

* * *

The preceding discussion refines the general theory and logic of coercive diplomacy. It identifies four "empty boxes" or critical variables imbedded in the abstract model that the policymaker must deal with in formulating and implementing any particular strategy of coercive diplomacy. A typology of four different variants of the strategy is presented. Attention is directed to relationships between key variables of the strategy—what is demanded of the opponent and how strongly motivated he is to resist such demands—in order to emphasize that such relationships have much to do with the balance of interests and relative motivation of the two sides, which help determine the effectiveness of the strategy in a particular situation.

However, even as refined and reformulated in the present study, the abstract model of coercive diplomacy is not a textbook of "how-to-do-it" prescriptions. The task of "operationalizing" the theory remains. The policymaker must judge which variant of the strategy—or indeed whether any variant of it—can be made to work in the situation at hand. This task is difficult because it requires the policymaker to understand and deal with a number of additional contextual variables that the abstract theory does not take into account. Such variables are identified in the case studies and discussed in Part Three.

part two

The Practice of Coercive Diplomacy
Case Studies

The abstract theory of coercive diplomacy presented in Part One can guide policymakers only to a limited extent. What is needed, in addition, is generic knowledge of how and why variants of coercive diplomacy do or do not work in practice, what challenges and obstacles the strategy can encounter, under what conditions it is likely to succeed or fail. Therefore, one must study historical experience with coercive persuasion to understand what it is about this phenomenon that the general theory has oversimplified or left out but that the policymaker ignores at his own peril. Studying the past practice of coercive diplomacy can provide us with a better understanding of the task that confronts policymakers when they consider adapting the general concept of coercive diplomacy to many different situations.

Accordingly, the purpose of Part Two is to provide case materials to construct generic knowledge of coercive diplomacy. Insights are obtained from analytic studies of historical cases in which policymakers used coercive diplomacy. Brief case studies are presented of seven instances in which the

United States employed some variant of coercive diplomacy in the post–World War II era. More detailed versions of most of these cases are, as indicated in the Bibliographical Note, available elsewhere. It should be understood that, as in the writing of history in general, the reconstruction of events and the interpretations offered in these case studies are provisional; new data and alternative interpretations may emerge in future scholarship that would require reconsideration of these case studies.

The seven cases differ strikingly in important respects: the magnitude of the objective the United States pursued by means of this strategy; the contexts in which the cases occurred; whether coercive diplomacy succeeded or failed. The diversity of the cases serves the purposes of the study very well in that it enables us to understand the problems of operationalizing the general strategy of coercive diplomacy and adapting it to different circumstances. The cases also provide a basis for understanding why policymakers employ different variants of the strategy in different circumstances, why the strategy is sometimes successful and sometimes unsuccessful. Each case provides information that is useful for developing generic knowledge. A similar set of questions is asked about each case; the answers serve as "building blocks" for the construction of generic knowledge.[1]

In no sense do these seven cases constitute a representative sample of all of the many historical instances in which the strategy was attempted and, therefore, one cannot extrapolate from them the probability of success of future attempts at coercive diplomacy.[2] What the seven cases do very well is provide a basis for understanding the context-dependent nature of the strategy, the conditions that favor success, the obstacles that may be encountered, and, more generally, the uses and limitations of the strategy.

All this information should be an aid to the judgment policymakers must exercise in determining whether this strategy is likely to be a viable option for dealing with different

kinds of encroachments that arise in the future. Quite obviously, coercive diplomacy is not the only option for dealing
with such encroachments. There are many cases in which
American policymakers decided not to resort to this strategy,
evidently sensing that it would be inappropriate, ineffectual,
or too risky.[3]

1. United States–Japan Relations
Leading to Pearl Harbor
Coercive Diplomacy That Boomeranged

It is sometimes assumed that the strategy of coercive diplomacy is certain to succeed if only the demands one makes on an opponent, however far-reaching they are, are backed by an unmistakably credible threat of severe punishment. The case of U.S.-Japanese relations leading to Pearl Harbor reveals that this assumption rests on a dangerously oversimplified and distorted understanding of coercive diplomacy and that it ignores some of the most important risks of the strategy. In fact, the oil embargo the United States imposed on Japan in July 1941 was so credible and so potent that it quickly provoked Japanese leaders into making a very difficult and desperate decision to initiate war rather than capitulate to Washington's extreme demands that it get out of China and, in effect, give up its aspirations for regional hegemony in Southeast Asia.

The oil embargo was not only very damaging to Japan; in effect it created an urgent time limit for compliance with U.S.

demands. Japan imported 80 percent of its fuel supplies from the United States and had been unable to develop alternative sources of supply. In September 1941 Japanese leaders concluded that they must decide by October whether to accept a negotiated settlement with the United States, if acceptable terms could be obtained, or to initiate war while Japan still had sufficient oil to wage it. Thus, although economic sanctions have often proven too weak as an instrument of diplomacy, in this case they failed, ironically, because they were all too potent!

One might ask whether coercive diplomacy boomeranged because American leaders were unaware of the crippling effect an oil embargo would have on Japan's military capability. This was not the case. President Roosevelt had pursued a cautious policy of pressure on Japan for some time prior to July because he and his advisers were fully aware of Japan's acute dependence on importing oil from the United States. Roosevelt was concerned lest shutting off oil to Japan force it to move against the Dutch East Indies in order to acquire oil. Accordingly, Roosevelt backed off from imposing an oil embargo and chose the safer option of employing it as a deterrent threat to dissuade Japan from further aggressive moves in Asia.

As U.S. policy developed over time, however, the threat of an oil embargo as part of a deterrent strategy was transformed into actual imposition of a full-scale oil embargo as the instrument of a highly ambitious strategy of coercive diplomacy.

It is often stated that the effort to deter Japan from further moves into Southeast Asia failed and that, therefore, Pearl Harbor illustrates the limitations of deterrence strategy. What this statement of the "lesson" fails to grasp, however, is that the United States added to its ongoing deterrence effort an extremely ambitious use of the strategy of coercive diplomacy. In other words, Pearl Harbor is not a simple case of deterrence failure. It is, rather, a case in which coercive diplomacy provoked the adversary into a decision for war. Deterrence aims at dissuading an adversary from doing something he hasn't as yet done. By contrast, the object of coercive diplomacy is to induce an adversary to stop or undo a course of action on which he is already embarked.

We need not trace in detail the development of U.S.-Japanese relations in the years leading to Pearl Harbor. Suffice it to observe that Washington's policy gradually hardened, embracing more ambitious objectives and more severe means of achieving them. To the objective of deterring further Japanese aggression was eventually added the much more ambitious objective of forcing Japan to withdraw from China and, in effect, to give up its aspirations for achieving a Greater East-Asia Co-Prosperity Sphere.

What this case illustrates is that the strategies of deterrence and coercive diplomacy are highly context-dependent, that contextual conditions can change over time in ways that make the success of deterrence and coercive diplomacy increasingly problematic, and that domestic politics, international political constraints, and bureaucratic struggles over policy on both sides can severely handicap the search for a peaceful settlement.

American policymakers seem never to have faced the implications of the fact that the stakes in Asia were clearly greater for Japan than for the United States. Instead, Washington steadily sharpened its terms for a diplomatic settlement, thereby strengthening even more Japan's motivation to resist. The underlying assumption of Washington's policy—until the end, when highly classified intelligence sources revealed that Japan's desperate choice was to initiate war rather than accept American demands—was that Japan's leaders would knuckle under rather than accept war with an enemy whose military-economic power and potential were vastly greater than its own. When this assumption was called into question during the last-minute negotiations at the end of November, Washington refused to moderate its demands on Japan or to offer a larger carrot. Roosevelt perceived and accepted the likelihood of war. In the last few days it was evident that Japan would launch war; the surprise lay only in the Japanese attack on Pearl Harbor. The ambitious objective of the coercive diplomacy pursued by the United States had backed the Japanese government into a corner without leaving it an acceptable way out. With its highest imperialist aspirations at stake, the Japanese government chose the desperate, low-confidence strategy of war with the United States, for it perceived the only alternative as even less acceptable.

It should be noted, too, that the variant of coercive diplomacy Washington applied relied almost exclusively on a heavy "stick"—the oil embargo—and made scant use of "carrots" to make its demands more acceptable. The final diplomatic effort, in November 1941, to explore a possible compromise failed when it became clear that the irreducible positions of the two sides remained far apart and could not be bridged by the minor concessions each was willing to make at that stage. By November 1941 the course of events had greatly weakened the voices of moderates on both sides, playing into the hands of those who favored an unyielding position.

In reflecting on the nature of Japanese imperialistic ambitions and America's emerging conception of its own global interests and its strategic conceptions, one might conclude that a war between the two countries was inevitable and that historical developments leading to Pearl Harbor merely determined the timing and circumstances of such a war. Some would even argue that, however costly the war with Japan proved to be, it was necessary in order to eliminate Japan as a militaristic, imperialistic power. We need not debate this proposition here in order to call attention to the narrower set of lessons this case provides regarding problems that the strategy of coercive diplomacy can encounter and the conditions under which, instead of providing a peaceful alternative, the strong ultimatum variant of the strategy can boomerang and provoke war. Besides, it should be noted that at the beginning of their prolonged diplomatic crisis and for some time thereafter, neither Japanese nor American leaders believed that their disagreement would or should lead to war. Developments in U.S.-Japanese relations between 1938 and 1941 are replete with instances of misperception and miscalculation, failure to convey clear commitment and to send consistent signals, and inability to understand each other's perspective. The result was that the dispute assumed an escalatory dynamic beyond the control of either side, and war became inevitable.

2. The Laos Crisis of 1961–62
Coercive Diplomacy for Minimal Objectives

In the prolonged Laotian crisis of 1961–62 President Kennedy eventually employed coercive diplomacy successfully on behalf of quite limited objectives. Shortly after assuming office in January 1961, Kennedy concluded that the United States was seriously overextended in Laos. Confronted by the prospect that the civil war in that country would result in the military defeat and collapse of the Royal Lao government that the United States was backing, the president decided against direct military intervention by U.S. forces and chose instead to cut his losses. Kennedy abandoned the American objective of establishing a stable noncommunist government in the entire kingdom. He decided instead to settle for the much more limited objective of preventing an overrunning of key positions of the Royal Lao government by Pathet Lao forces that were being supplied by the Soviet Union, China, and North Vietnam, and to seek their acceptance of a neutralized Laos.

Although his objective was limited, Kennedy attached considerable importance to achieving it. Laos itself was not of

intrinsic value, but Kennedy inherited a commitment made
by his predecessor that had led to an extraordinary American involvement in the affairs of that small country. Laos was
due protection under the umbrella of the Southeast Asia
Treaty Organization created by Eisenhower and Dulles after
the Korean War to protect Southeast Asia from Chinese
communist aggression. Because Laos had common borders
with the noncommunist states of Thailand, South Vietnam,
Cambodia, and Burma, it had assumed considerable strategic, political, and psychological importance for American
policy in the region. Although it was President Eisenhower
who had coined the phrase "row of dominoes" to emphasize
the interconnectedness of American commitments and the
possible ramifications elsewhere of a setback in any one lo-
cale, Kennedy was sensitive to the same considerations. He
had to contend with a Thai government that anxiously con-
templated the increased threat to its security that a communist regime in Laos would pose. The president and his advisers were also aware that the outcome in Laos would affect the
security and defense of South Vietnam. These and other
considerations lent urgency to Kennedy's effort to salvage as
much as possible, to prevent a complete overrunning of Laos
and to achieve its neutralization.

Thus, Kennedy had ample incentive to avoid a humiliating
setback in Laos and to achieve his limited objective. He was
strongly enough motivated, if not to intervene militarily,
then at least to generate threats of military intervention that
would be credible enough to make the desired impression on
his opponents. However, even Kennedy's shrunken objective
proved enormously difficult to realize. The forces of the
Royal Lao government did poorly in the field despite the
flow of supplies from Washington. Kennedy repeatedly was
forced to threaten intervention in order to discourage the
Pathet Lao forces from pressing their advantage on the
battlefield too far. The president attempted to induce acceptance of his minimal demand for a cease-fire and constitution

of a neutralist government by means of a try-and-see variant of coercive diplomacy. Wishing to avoid U.S. military involvement and actions that might be provocative, the president took one small diplomatic step at a time and, as it proved insufficient, reluctantly took another.

The "carrot" Kennedy offered (U.S. disengagement from Laos in favor of neutralization) was a substantial one, but it proved insufficient. The task of coercive diplomacy in this case was complicated because the opponent was not a single country but a multinational coalition. The three communist states backing the Pathet Lao disagreed among themselves on how to respond to Kennedy's offer and what conditions to attach to its acceptance. The Soviet Union, China, and North Vietnam basically agreed on the objective of making Laos a communist state, but they differed in their willingness to accept costs and risks on behalf of this goal. In the end it was Kennedy's ability to discern and exploit these differences that enabled him to succeed.

The Soviets were the chief supplier of arms to the Pathet Lao, but given their distance from the scene and their greater interests elsewhere, they were not willing to pay a high price or take substantial risks on behalf of an immediate communist takeover of Laos. Neither Khrushchev nor Kennedy wanted a major imbroglio over Laos to complicate their efforts to deal with more important issues in U.S.-Soviet relations. At the same time, however, Moscow could not easily back off, as to do so might show it to be less committed than China to the support of national liberation movements. In fact, the considerable military and economic aid the Soviet Union had been giving the Pathet Lao for some time may well have been driven by its desire to compete with Peking for the allegiance of Hanoi.

Kennedy failed to make progress with his initial try-and-see approach, which relied so heavily on the concession he was willing to offer. It became clear to him that the carrot would have to be supplemented by a stronger stick. Faced by a deteriorating, highly unstable situation in Laos, Kennedy felt compelled by mid-March to add a threat of military intervention and to create some sense of urgency for compliance with his demand. He ordered troop preparations and preliminary movements for possible deployment of American troops into Thailand, where they would be ready to intervene in Laos. This effort to strengthen his coercive diplomacy strategy was not accompanied by an explicit time limit for compliance with his demand for a cease-fire. However, Kennedy did warn that U.S. forces would intervene if the Pathet Lao forces threatened to overrun areas critical to the survival of the Royal Lao government, and perhaps this warning substituted sufficiently for a time limit to give his strategy the character of a tacit ultimatum. Indeed, the Pathet Lao decided to avoid attacking towns in the sensitive Mekong Valley, concentrating instead on consolidating and extending its control elsewhere.

At the same time that he converted his earlier try-and-see approach to the equivalent of a tacit ultimatum, Kennedy increased the attractiveness of his proposal by finally accepting the Communist demand for an international conference to work out a settlement. Kennedy's acceptance, however, was made conditional on prior achievement of a verified cease-fire in Laos. Although strengthened and made more attractive, this new version of the president's strategy remained unsuccessful for the time being.

It had become evident to Washington that the Soviet Union would be pivotal to the success of Kennedy's strategy. There was reason to believe that Moscow would find the proposal for neutralization of Laos attractive and that it was sensitive enough to the threat of U.S. military intervention to be swayed to work for a peaceful settlement. Khrushchev indeed conveyed interest in the formula for a neutral Laos but had to contend with his allies. Faced with Washington's insistence on a cease-fire as a condition for an international conference, Khrushchev was stymied by China's opposition to a cease-fire and its seeming determination to show up Moscow as being weaker in its revolutionary ardor than Peking. Khrushchev apparently tried, although without success, to circumvent Chinese resistance by gaining support for a verified preconference cease-fire from Hanoi and the Viet Minh. But there appeared to be limits beyond which Moscow would not go in pressing its allies, and meanwhile the military situation in Laos continued to deteriorate.

At this point, early in April, the president was confronted by the failure of the Bay of Pigs invasion and became worried that his decision not to back the Cuban exile force with American military action might be taken as a sign of U.S. irresolution in Laos as well. Accordingly, he ordered the four hundred U.S. "civilian advisers" in Laos to put on their military uniforms and join Royal Lao army units at the front line. By accepting the risk of casualties to U.S. soldiers, a development that presumably might lead to escalation of U.S. intervention, Kennedy hoped to make his threat of a larger military intervention credible and persuasive.

This was indeed a small step, but it fit the characteristics of an "exemplary action" that the general theory of coercive diplomacy holds to be effective under some circumstances for strengthening the credibility and impact of coercive threats. The move did seem to help persuade Hanoi and Peking to accept a British-Soviet plan for a cease-fire and the call for an international conference. However, the Pathet Lao accelerated its offensive action as if to gain as much as possible before a cease-fire took effect, a development that forced Washington once again to give serious consideration to intervention. In the end Kennedy rejected plans for intervention in Laos, deciding that if a military stand had to be made it would be better to do so in Thailand or in South Vietnam, where the indigenous forces seemed more willing and able to fight effectively. The president also took steps to limit the international and domestic costs of his decision. At the same time, the president placed a marine division on alert at Okinawa, readying it for possible deployment into Thailand, and increased diplomatic pressure on the Soviet Union to help bring about a cease-fire before Laos was overrun by Pathet Lao forces. Some uncertainty remained as to whether and at what point the president might commit combat forces into Laos, and his advisers were divided on the matter.

Fortunately, the Pathet Lao and Royal Lao government reached agreement on cease-fire terms and fighting dwindled, clearing the way for the international conference in mid-May. At their summit meeting in Vienna in early June, Kennedy and Khrushchev agreed to cooperate in bringing about neutralization of Laos. After many months of negotiations, renewed fighting in Laos, and a movement of substantial U.S. forces into Thailand, the Geneva conference finally produced an agreement late in July 1962 that ratified in principle a de facto partition of Laos and set up a coalition government (that predictably proved to be weak and unstable).

Kennedy's success, therefore, was a modest one that fell short of achieving all of the quite limited objectives for Laos he had opted for at the beginning of his administration. The result was not a stable, independent Laotian government that, once its neutralization was agreed to, could hope to prevent Hanoi from continuing to use its territory for ferrying supplies down the Ho Chi Minh trail into South Vietnam. The most that can be said is that Kennedy avoided a worse outcome in Laos and gained time for further development of a policy for dealing with developments in the rest of Southeast Asia.

3. The Cuban Missile Crisis
Peaceful Resolution Through Coercive Diplomacy

The Soviet deployment of medium-range ballistic missiles into Cuba during the late summer and early fall of 1962 triggered the most dangerous crisis of the Cold War. This war-threatening confrontation, unforeseen and unwanted by either side, was eventually resolved peacefully through careful crisis management by both Washington and Moscow.

A peaceful outcome was possible because, instead of resorting to military action to destroy the missiles, President Kennedy decided to try the strategy of coercive diplomacy in an effort to induce Khrushchev to remove them. Although the naval blockade that the United States put into effect could prevent additional missiles and military equipment from reaching Cuba, it obviously could not remove the missiles that had already arrived and were being made operational. It was Kennedy's hope, however, that the blockade and preparations for a possible air strike or invasion of Cuba would demonstrate his resolution and exert enough pressure to induce Khrushchev to remove the missiles.

But would the Soviet leader challenge the naval blockade, which he denounced as an "act of war"? Would Soviet vessels and submarines attempt to pass through the blockade line and, if so, might this lead to a shooting war on the high seas or escalation elsewhere? There was no assurance that coercive diplomacy was a viable strategy or that it could be applied without setting into motion developments that would lead to war.

Kennedy initially employed the relatively weak try-and-see approach. He deliberately slowed implementation of the blockade, subdividing it into a series of small steps. And although the coercive impact of the try-and-see strategy was strengthened because the blockade was accompanied by an ominous build-up of U.S. military forces, the president deliberately steered clear during the first five days of the confrontation of giving Khrushchev a time limit for compliance with his demand for removal of the missiles and backing it with an explicit threat of an air strike or invasion for noncompliance.

In applying the strategy of coercive diplomacy the president also had to engage in careful crisis management, hoping that Khrushchev would do the same so that they could together try to end the confrontation before it escalated to war. Indeed, the president carefully observed relevant crisis management principles. Thus he limited his objective to removal of the missiles, rejecting advice that he use the crisis to get rid of Castro or at least eliminate Soviet influence in Cuba. Intuitively, Kennedy realized that to pursue these more ambitious goals would have greatly strengthened Soviet motivation, made coercive persuasion much more difficult, and increased the likelihood of war. In addition to limiting his objective, the president, as already noted, limited the means he employed. The blockade option appealed to Kennedy because it enabled him to initiate a showdown with Khrushchev without immediate resort to force and, most important, it offered him time to try persuading the Soviet leader to remove the missiles voluntarily.

The president also adhered to important operational principles of crisis management. He maintained informed presidential-level control over the movements of military forces; slowed the momentum of the crisis to enable both sides to consider their policy options and to give time for diplomatic communications; attempted to coordinate military and political actions to ensure clear and consistent signaling; accompanied his firm demand for removal of the missiles and his conduct of the blockade with a clear signal of his preference for a peaceful resolution of the crisis; and, finally, avoided boxing Khrushchev into a corner that might make him desperate enough to escalate the crisis in the hope of avoiding a humiliating defeat.

As for Khrushchev, even though he blustered and issued coercive threats of his own in an effort to undermine Kennedy's resolve, he nonetheless went to great lengths to avoid a clash at sea. Within hours after Kennedy announced the blockade on Monday evening, October 22, and well before Washington became aware of it, Khrushchev directed Soviet vessels carrying missiles and other military equipment to Cuba to turn back immediately. Other Soviet vessels carrying nonmilitary cargo temporarily halted and later resumed movement toward the blockade line to test and, if possible, weaken Kennedy's resolution to implement it. In addition, the Soviet leader placed heavy reliance, but to no avail, on efforts to persuade the president and the world of the legitimacy of his military assistance to Cuba and his claim that the missiles were "defensive."

Thus, both Khrushchev and Kennedy behaved with sober prudence and reasonable skill to extricate themselves from the war-threatening crisis. The danger of escalation to war did indeed cast an ominous pall over crisis developments. But although both leaders attempted to gain advantage through crisis bargaining and although their behavior evoked concern that they might be about to embark on a dangerous game of chicken on the high seas, in fact neither Kennedy nor Khrushchev engaged in a reckless competition in risk-taking but acted cautiously to avoid escalation.

Once the danger of a clash on the high seas was safely managed, however, U.S. and Soviet cooperation in managing the crisis began to break down. On Saturday morning, which was to become the last day of the confrontation, they suddenly experienced disturbing new challenges to their ability to control the escalation potential of the crisis. A startling lack of synchronization in the interaction between the two sides emerged. The context and meaning of possibly critical moves and communications became confusing; deciphering the intentions and calculations behind specific moves of the opponent became difficult. Policymakers in Washington puzzled over the discrepancy between Khrushchev's personal and emotional private letter of Friday evening, in which he hinted at a deal for withdrawal of the missiles in return for a U.S. pledge of noninvasion of Cuba, and his more formal letter of Saturday morning that advanced the additional demand for removal of U.S. Jupiter missiles from Turkey. Other disturbing events occurred on Saturday. A U-2 spy plane was shot down over Cuba; two other U.S. reconnaissance aircraft were shot at by Cuban air defense forces as they swooped low over the missile sites; a U.S. reconnaissance plane wandered over Siberia; reports came in that Soviet consulate personnel were burning classified papers. Confused by these developments, U.S. policymakers anxiously speculated that the Kremlin was now taking a harder line and was determined to test U.S. resolution, that Khrushchev was no longer in charge, or that Moscow was trying to extract a higher price for removal of the missiles.

The president and his advisers worried that the downing of the U-2 portended a major escalation of the crisis. Kennedy momentarily withstood pressures to retaliate via an air strike against a Soviet surface-to-air missile site in Cuba. But it was clear that U-2 reconnaissance flights over Cuba would have to continue in order to monitor activity at the missile sites and that if another U-2 were shot down, a development which had to be expected, the president could not continue to hold off reprisal. What would happen thereafter, he feared, could lead to uncontrollable military escalation.

A new sense of urgency to end the crisis emerged since it could be only a matter of days before another U-2 was shot down. An immediate effort to end the crisis before it went out of control was deemed necessary. To this end the president was finally ready, indeed now felt compelled, to exert much stronger pressure on Khrushchev. But at the same time, Kennedy believed it was necessary to couple the additional pressure with concessions to make it easier for the Soviet leader to agree to remove the missiles. Indeed, from an early stage in the crisis Kennedy had believed he would probably have to pay a price of some kind to get Khrushchev to pull out the missiles. But the president strongly felt that concessions should come not at the beginning of the bargaining, but only after he had fully impressed the Soviet leader with his determination and developed strong bargaining assets to reduce substantially his part of a quid pro quo.

Two important changes now took place in the president's strategy of coercive diplomacy. He finally converted his try-and-see approach into a virtual ultimatum. But at the same time he made the ultimatum part of a carrot-and-stick variant, adding concessions he had earlier refused to discuss. The president accepted the idea that Khrushchev had hinted at in his Friday letter, that a noninvasion pledge be given in return for removal of the missiles, and added to it a secret agreement to remove U.S. Jupiter missiles from Turkey. At the same time Kennedy conveyed the equivalent of an ultimatum by having his brother warn Soviet ambassador Dobrynin that the president had to have Khrushchev's acceptance of this offer within twenty-four hours because he would not be able to hold off taking stronger action much longer. The substance of this time-urgent ultimatum was conveyed in other ways as well; preparations for an invasion of Cuba had been completed on the same day, and Soviet and Cuban intelligence appear to have warned Moscow that American military action was imminent.

Some of the disturbing developments of Saturday, October 27, had a profoundly unsettling effect on Khrushchev as well, in particular the U-2 shoot-down, which Soviet commanders in Cuba undertook without explicit orders from Moscow. Evidently Khrushchev, too, feared that the crisis was getting out of control and that American military action could be expected shortly. Within a few hours he accepted Kennedy's formula for settling the crisis. What would the president have done if Khrushchev had refused? Evidence suggests that Kennedy would not have gone immediately to military action against Cuba but would have further tightened the blockade and possibly made the additional concession of a public agreement to remove the Jupiters from Turkey.

The strategy of coercive diplomacy, therefore, did work in this case. It worked because Kennedy limited his objective and the means he employed on its behalf. Whether it would have worked had Kennedy not made the concessions he did is arguable. Adherence to crisis management principles by both sides was of critical importance. Critical, too, was Kennedy's success in convincing Khrushchev that the United States was more highly motivated by what was at stake than was the Soviet Union—that is, that it was more important to the United States to get the missiles out of Cuba than it was to the Soviet Union to keep them there—and that he had the resolution to achieve that objective.

A number of other factors that contributed to the peaceful resolution of this crisis will not necessarily be present in other war-threatening confrontations. Absent from this crisis was the occurrence of a serious miscalculation or incident that might have triggered unwanted escalation. The image of thermonuclear war shared by the two leaders created powerful incentives on both sides to manage and terminate the crisis peacefully. Opportunities for avoiding escalation were available; they were highly valued and carefully cultivated by both leaders. The two leaders operated with sufficient understanding of the requirements of crisis management and with adequate skill to bring the confrontation to a close without being drawn into a war. However, several serious threats to effective crisis management did occur. Foremost among them were the downing of the U-2 and aggressive antisubmarine activities of the U.S. Navy, which pursued all five Soviet submarines in the area and forced them to surface, an activity that might have led to serious incidents between the forces. Under different circumstances either of these two developments might have triggered escalation to a war.

Finally, we must note that the images Kennedy and Khrushchev held of each other played an important role in the inception and resolution of the crisis. Just as Khrushchev's *defective* image of Kennedy—as a young, inexperienced leader who could be pushed around and who was too weak or too "rational" to risk war to get the missiles out— played a role in his decision to deploy the missiles, so did Kennedy's *correct* image of Khrushchev as a rational, intelligent man who would retreat if given sufficient time and shown resolution play a critical role in the president's choice of the strategy of coercive diplomacy and his determination to give it a chance to succeed.

One would like to believe that fateful questions of war and peace are not influenced by subjective, psychological variables of this kind. However, a full understanding of the missile crisis is not possible without taking into account the personalities of the two leaders and the personal aspects of their interaction. Coercive diplomacy was successful in this case because of the special conditions we have identified. There is no guarantee that conditions favoring coercive diplomacy will be present in other war-threatening confrontations.

4. Vietnam 1965

The Failure of Air Power to Coerce Hanoi

By early 1965 the political-military position of the South Vietnam government had gradually deteriorated and it had reached the point of near collapse. Frustrated by its inability to find ways to develop a stable government in Saigon and more effective South Vietnamese military resistance to the Viet Cong, the United States found itself with the grim alternatives of withdrawal or some form of military intervention. Rejecting disengagement, Washington was confronted by the immediate need to reaffirm its commitment and to demonstrate resolution to prevent a Viet Cong and North Vietnamese victory. The Johnson administration's decision was to prepare for a retaliatory air strike against targets in North Vietnam in response to the next Viet Cong attack on U.S. military installations in South Vietnam. To do so was considered all the more urgent because Washington had failed to retaliate for two recent Viet Cong attacks on U.S. military installations. After the first reprisal strike, a decision was made to undertake sustained air operations against North Vietnam, not in retaliation for specific provocations, but as a more general response to continuing North Vietnamese intervention in South Vietnam.

Two retaliatory air attacks were made on February 7 and 11 in response to Viet Cong attacks on a U.S. helicopter base at Pleiku and a U.S. enlisted men's barracks at Qui Non. And, after some delay, which gave the State Department time to issue a White Paper documenting Hanoi's role in aiding and directing the guerrilla war against the government of South Vietnam, the second stage of continuing air strikes was initiated on March 2.

There were several reasons for the cautious way President Johnson eased the United States into direct military intervention. He had ample reason to be concerned over lack of domestic support for intervention and also had to contend with considerable opposition to it among many allied nations and neutral governments. Also, the president worried lest direct U.S. military intervention provoke Hanoi to counterescalate with greater involvement of its own and have an undesirable impact on the Soviets and the Chinese. For all these reasons, until mid-March the president was much more concerned with managing the risks of direct U.S. military intervention than with seriously attempting to enhance its coercive impact on Hanoi. Indeed, although the administration stated that these occasional air strikes were to put pressure on Hanoi, they were motivated more by a desire to shore up Saigon's morale than to initiate a strategy of coercive diplomacy.

In response to recommendations from his military advisers, on March 15 the president approved more frequent, larger air strikes, and these now became part of a more deliberate but, as it turned out, rather weak effort to coerce Hanoi into abandoning its aid to the Viet Cong. Official statements from Washington said only that the air attacks were being undertaken because of Hanoi's "continued acts of aggression" against South Vietnam, but press reports made it clear that they were intended to remind Hanoi that it would incur increasing punishment if it persisted.[4] U.S. and South Vietnamese aircraft launched attacks almost daily against radar stations, supply depots, barracks, small bridges, and targets of opportunity along North Vietnamese highways and railroads. However, these bombing missions were deliberately restricted to a limited area north of the 17th parallel that divided South and North Vietnam, and extended no closer than approximately one hundred miles from the Hanoi-Haiphong area. Moreover, again as a matter of policy, the air strikes were targeted almost exclusively against North Vietnam's transportation system and its lines of supply and communication to South Vietnam. The exceptions were two strikes early in April, against major highway and railway bridges sixty-five and seventy-two miles south of Hanoi and against a thermal power plant, the latter being the only purely industrial target attacked in the first four months of the air war.

It should be noted that this pattern of bombing was endorsed by the president's military advisers. Until March the Joint Chiefs of Staff and the military commands had consistently advocated a harsh, intensive bombing campaign as offering greater coercive potential against Hanoi. Late in February, however, as the Viet Cong showed signs of consolidating their resources for a major offensive, the advice of U.S. military leaders began to shift to greater emphasis on air attacks against interdiction targets to disrupt the flow of military supplies to the Viet Cong. Dealing with the threat on the ground in South Vietnam began to assume priority over using air power against other targets in North Vietnam to increase coercive pressure on Hanoi. This policy was strongly reaffirmed at the important meeting of the president's advisers in Honolulu on April 20. They agreed that the program of air strikes should continue essentially as it had developed, with emphasis on interdiction targets. As for high-value targets in the Hanoi–Haiphong–Phuc Yen areas, most participants in the Honolulu meeting agreed that they were to be avoided for the time being and held hostage for later when bargaining for a settlement might get underway. It was clear that the administration had come to believe that it would have to rely on making progress in the war in South Vietnam rather than on coercive air bombing to erode Hanoi's will. Washington's strategy had shifted from the initial try-and-see variant of coercive diplomacy to the quite different strategy of military attrition in the south.

Why, one may ask, had not a much stronger air campaign been undertaken earlier on behalf of a more potent coercive diplomacy? As noted earlier, from the beginning of American military intervention in February, political-diplomatic reasons dictated considerable restraint in the use of air power as a coercive instrument. Mention has already been made of President Johnson's concern not to intervene militarily in ways that might be provocative and of his efforts to manage the risks of the intervention. Washington's concern lest heavy air attacks against North Vietnam provoke the Soviet Union derived from the fact that Moscow had publicly agreed to provide North Vietnam with military assistance. Following Khrushchev's ouster in October 1964, Soviet policy toward Vietnam hardened and arrangements were made to send much more assistance to Hanoi. On several occasions during late December and January, Soviet spokesmen pledged to come to the aid of Hanoi if the United States extended the war to its territory. In this respect Moscow's policy was influenced by its struggle with the Chinese for global leadership of communist-oriented revolutionary movements.

Nonetheless, the desperate situation he faced in Vietnam encouraged Johnson to cling to the hope that Moscow, if not provoked, might once again, as in the earlier Laotian crisis, play a pivotal role in persuading Hanoi and China to dampen tendencies to escalate the conflict. Johnson took special pains to assure the Soviet Union of his desire to avoid a wider war in Southeast Asia, even while conveying determination to take steps as necessary to stop Hanoi's continuing aggression against South Vietnam.

The Soviet Union seemed to lend encouragement to such hopes in mid-February when it indicated to the British government that it was interested in taking an active role in arranging a peaceful settlement. On February 23, the Soviet government publicly declared its support for a negotiated settlement through reconvening the Geneva conference. However, this announcement by no means constituted assurance that Moscow was prepared to influence Hanoi to give up its aims in the south. More plausibly, Moscow may have been ready to arrange for Johnson, as it had for Kennedy, a face-saving way out of the situation.

It is instructive to consider why Johnson, unlike Kennedy, was unable to persuade Moscow to play a pivotal diplomatic role. Both presidents faced losing, indeed desperate, situations. But whereas Kennedy had decided against military intervention and moved to cut his losses by expressing a willingness to settle for neutralization of Laos, Johnson initiated direct American military intervention and made it clear that the United States would not retreat from its commitment to South Vietnam.

Kennedy had used the threat of U.S. military intervention as leverage to activate the Soviets into persuading the other communist states to go along with his proposal for neutralization of Laos. Johnson's effort to apply coercive diplomacy in a similar manner to manipulate the multistate opposition did not succeed. It is important to note that Johnson felt compelled—as Kennedy had in Laos—to observe the requirements of crisis management in pursuing this intricate diplomatic-military strategy. The president thought that limiting the application of air power to carefully measured, discrete doses was essential to enable Moscow to exercise its influence with the other communist actors. According to this reasoning, the president should apply just enough force—without pressing too hard—to make credible the threat of severely punishing North Vietnam if it did not comply. Johnson hoped this policy would motivate Moscow and at the same time allow it to play a pivotal role. Restraint in the air campaign against North Vietnam was deemed necessary for other reasons as well. Hanoi should be intimidated but not damaged so much by U.S. air power that it would be driven into the arms of Communist China. Washington feared that China would intervene on a large scale, as it had after U.S. forces moved into North Korea, if American military pressure on Hanoi were too great. The lesson of Korea was not forgotten in Washington, and Johnson was not disposed to accept any risk of Chinese intervention.

All these factors constituted an extremely delicate set of balances for Washington to orchestrate, more so than earlier in Laos. Why was Johnson's task more difficult than Kennedy's had been? Much more was at stake for Hanoi this time. In the Laos case Hanoi placed a greater priority on achieving its objective in South Vietnam, so it was unwilling to risk war with the United States over Laos in the face of Kennedy's credible threat of intervention. Besides, Hanoi could afford to accommodate Kennedy because he was engaged in a partial disengagement from Laos that did not jeopardize Hanoi's essential interests in that country. In the Vietnam case, Johnson's demands on Hanoi were much more onerous than the modest objective Kennedy pursued in 1961. In 1965 Hanoi was on the verge of finally achieving its long-standing national goals in what it regarded as a civil war to unify the two parts of its country. It was much more strongly motivated to resist Johnson's demand that it give up *this* objective than it had been to oppose Kennedy's demand for a neutralized Laos.

In effect, therefore, Johnson's far-reaching objectives and demands made it much more difficult for the Soviet Union to play the same role it had in 1961 and, more generally, made the task of coercive diplomacy overwhelmingly difficult. Indeed it is hardly surprising that Johnson failed to coerce Hanoi; it would have been far more surprising had he succeeded. The situation Washington faced was only superficially similar to that in the Laos case. The conditions for the strongest form of coercive diplomacy simply were not present. Thus, although the United States was strongly motivated by what was at stake, its demand that Hanoi give up its aspiration to unify Vietnam under its own political system strongly increased Hanoi's determination to resist and, if anything, created an asymmetry of motivation in its favor.

Another condition that favors coercive diplomacy—a sense of urgency for compliance with the demand—was also missing. The air campaign waged against North Vietnam did not attempt to convey a sense of urgency to Hanoi. In its signals to Hanoi the administration stopped well short of stipulating or implying a time limit for compliance or, for that matter, threatening overwhelming punishment for non-compliance. In sum, the administration's mild try-and-see variant of coercive diplomacy was never converted into a tacit or explicit ultimatum. Indeed, some American policymakers had long believed that Hanoi was not coercible by such means.

We have already reviewed the reasons why Johnson held back from undertaking a stronger air campaign. It is arguable whether, had these political-diplomatic constraints not prevailed, powerful air attacks against targets that constituted North Vietnam's most important assets could have coerced Hanoi into changing its policy.

Finally, it should be noted that the conflict of interests between the two sides in this case approximated a zero-sum contest. Unlike the Laos case, there was little room in this crisis for a negotiated compromise. To the extent that Johnson did employ the strategy of coercive diplomacy, it was one in which there could be little if any scope for genuine negotiation. Johnson relied on threats and could offer next to no positive inducements to gain Hanoi's acquiescense. Thus in February and March of 1965, when the Soviets and British raised the possibility of reconvening the Geneva conference with the aim of negotiating a settlement, the administration rejected the idea. Secretary of State Rusk emphasized that negotiation would be futile as long as Hanoi had not first indicated its readiness to halt its direction and support of the Viet Cong. The administration was most reluctant to enter into any negotiations, as to do so might further demoralize the Saigon government that was struggling to deal with the precarious situation in South Vietnam. Later, domestic and international pressure mounted on the administration to develop a negotiating position. Seventeen nonaligned nations issued a statement urging a negotiated settlement. At home the influential columnist Walter Lippmann strongly criticized the administration's policy of "all stick and no carrot," and numerous voices called on the administration to undertake a negotiating initiative. The president responded with a major speech at Johns Hopkins University on April 7 in which he stressed his desire for "unconditional *discussions*" (a phrase we emphasize here to note that it deliberately avoided a commitment to "negotiations"). To the stick of air attacks the president now added for the first time a carrot: a spectacular offer of a major economic development plan for the entire Mekong River basin, from which North Vietnam could benefit. Johnson stated that he would ask Congress for a one billion dollar appropriation to help finance the project once the nations of Southeast Asia agreed to participate. Although Johnson's personal commitment to a TVA-like development project for Southeast Asia has been shown to be sincere, the administration's readiness to negotiate a settlement at the time is highly questionable. In fact, Washington privately expected the war to continue for some time to come; the main purpose of the Johns Hopkins speech was to dampen the growing criticism of the administration's policy. Aware that the speech did not really signal a change in Washington's objectives, Hanoi and Moscow quickly turned down the proposal. A few months later, the president made his fateful decision to begin the large-scale introduction of ground combat forces.

5. The Reagan Administration's Use of Coercive Diplomacy Against Nicaragua

The Reagan administration came into office in January 1981 determined to prevent the Sandinista regime in Nicaragua from continuing to ship arms to the guerrillas in El Salvador. This was a quite limited though important objective to pursue in relations with Nicaragua's Marxist-oriented government. In the following years Washington escalated both the objective and the means it employed in its strategy of coercive diplomacy against the Nicaraguan government. Initially the administration pursued quite limited objectives designed to contain the further spread of Marxist-oriented revolution in Central America and employed a mild carrot-and-stick variant of coercive diplomacy to this end. There were early indications that this objective could be achieved through an agreement with the Sandinista regime, but that possibility evaporated during the course of a pronounced struggle over policy within the Reagan administration. As a result, the administration's policy toward Nicaragua lacked clarity and consistency, and it drifted into a sterner version of coercive diplomacy aimed at the much more ambitious objective of destabilizing and replacing the Sandinista regime by means of economic sanctions and the creation of the Contra guerrilla army to overthrow it.

The hardening of U.S. policy toward Nicaragua aroused the concern of Latin American leaders who feared that it would lead to American military intervention in Central America. Beginning in 1982 they undertook a series of diplomatic initiatives to forestall further escalation of the conflict and to achieve a peaceful resolution that would promote regional stability and security. Eventually these efforts, largely opposed by hard-liners in the Reagan administration, led to free elections in Nicaragua early in 1989. The unexpected result was that the coalition candidate for the presidency, Violetta Chamorro, defeated the incumbent, Sandinista leader Daniel Ortega. This favorable development enabled George Bush, who shortly after becoming president had tacitly acknowledged the failure of the policy of relying on the Contras to bring about a change of regime in Nicaragua, to move to normalize relations with the new Nicaraguan government.

Although Washington's effort to coerce Nicaragua became intertwined with the competing efforts of the Central American states to resolve the conflict in their own way, it is useful for our purposes to focus on the unilateral U.S. effort at coercive diplomacy in order to identify factors that limited its effectiveness. The first factor was the lack of clear, consistent objectives for the policy toward Nicaragua. President Reagan's failure to set and enforce a clear policy line led to an intense struggle within his administration over the objectives and modalities of the policy. Administration hard-liners favored eliminating Sandinista rule in Nicaragua and opposed efforts of other members of the administration to offer positive incentives to induce the Sandinistas to respect U.S. security interests in Central America and to liberalize their regime. While those who favored a more moderate policy

wanted to use a carrot-and-stick approach to reach an accommodation with a more liberalized Sandinista regime, these
hard-liners rejected any approach that would combine positive incentives with coercion. Although the administration
described its policy as a "two-track" approach that combined
coercive pressure with efforts at negotiation, in practice this
approach could not be effectively implemented because of
the fundamental intra-administration disagreement over
policy objectives. Both the hard-liners and the moderates
agreed that coercive pressure needed to be applied. But the
moderates viewed such pressure as providing leverage for
serious diplomatic bargaining to extract concessions from
the Sandinistas, whereas the hard-liners viewed negotiations,
if any, as something to be manipulated and exploited to de-
pict the Sandinistas in a bad light in order to justify contin-
uation and possible escalation of coercive pressure and to obtain additional support for the Contras from Congress.

A second factor that worked against the success of coercive
diplomacy was that the objective of destabilizing and eliminating the Sandinistas served, not surprisingly, to strengthen
their motivation to resist. Coercive diplomacy is more likely
to succeed when the coercing state is more strongly motivated by what is at stake than its opponent. But the hard-
liners' threat to the Sandinista regime created the opposite
situation: an asymmetry of motivation in its favor that helped
compensate for its military and economic inferiority.

A third factor that undermined the Reagan administration's effort at coercive diplomacy was the lack of adequate
domestic and international support for the objectives and
modalities of its policy. Despite the administration's effort to
portray the Sandinistas as a threat to vital U.S. interests,
much of the public and many members of Congress were
not swayed. As a result, the administration had to struggle
repeatedly to obtain funds from Congress to continue support of the Contras. In fact, the absence of sufficient, sustained congressional support drove the administration to

seek alternative sources of funds, a risky policy gambit that backfired when the Iran-Contra scandal erupted.

Still another limiting factor was that the administration could not convey to the Sandinista leaders a sense of urgency for compliance with its demands. The variants of coercive diplomacy Washington employed were the weaker try-and-see and gradual turning of the screw approaches which, unlike the stronger ultimatum variant, convey no time limit for compliance.

Another condition that favors coercive diplomacy was missing in this case. The success of the strategy often depends on the ability to generate credible threats of additional punishment for continued noncompliance with one's demands. But this ability requires that the coercing power have additional usable options at its disposal; without them, threats of escalation lack credibility. As so often happens when strong powers attempt to intimidate weaker opponents, the Reagan administration could not convert its overwhelming superiority in military capabilities into usable options. Occasionally there were hints that U.S. naval and air power might be brought into play against Nicaragua, but when the covert mining of Nicaragua's harbors by the Central Intelligence Agency received publicity it triggered strong domestic and international condemnation. And, cognizant of the widespread concern in the country about another Vietnam-type involvement, the administration made no serious effort to threaten an invasion of Nicaragua by U.S. ground forces. The farthest it was willing to go in this direction was to argue that if congressional support for the Contras was not forthcoming, the administration might be forced to consider deploying American military forces. In the end, the administration was forced to fall back on a lesser combination of coercive pressures—economic sanctions (whose impact on Nicaragua was lessened by assistance it received from Soviet and other sources), the limited impact of the Contras, and various covert activities. As a result, the try-and-see approach was further diluted and came to resemble a prolonged war of attrition against the Sandinista regime.

Despite all these constraints, the coercive economic measures undertaken by the Reagan administration against Nicaragua did play an important role in wearing down its economy and weakening the Sandinista regime politically. Having to fight the Contras further exacerbated the economic problems of the regime and, by leading the regime to undertake further repressive measures, added to its domestic political difficulties as well. Support for the war among the Nicaraguan people eroded, and the combination of all these developments and the very real possibility of declining international support made Sandinista leaders more receptive to the negotiated settlement of the conflict that was being promoted by its regional neighbors.

In sum, the Reagan administration's coercive pressures against Nicaragua had the unanticipated indirect effect of stimulating a remarkable cooperative effort by Central American governments, one that Washington repeatedly attempted to undermine. It effectively constrained Washington and shielded Nicaragua from more drastic coercive pressures even while attempting to mediate the conflict. The Central American leaders developed their own framework for resolution of the conflict and eventually succeeded in inducing the Sandinistas to cooperate with it, a process that led to the unexpected electoral defeat of the Sandinistas. Ironically, in the end the United States achieved partial success in its effort to displace the Sandinista regime even though its attempts to achieve this objective through the Contra war were stymied by domestic political constraints and by the actions of the Central American states. But the partial success of American policy carried an enormous price tag. As a result of Washington's coercive economic pressures against the Sandinista regime, the new Nicaraguan government was left with an enormous task of rebuilding its economy in the interest of creating a stable democracy.

6. U.S. Coercive Diplomacy Against Libyan-Inspired Terrorism, December 1985–April 1986

Throughout its tenure the Reagan administration conducted a sporadic coercive campaign against Libya's Colonel Gaddafi in an effort to induce him to end his support of terrorism and moderate his generally provocative foreign policies. Following a series of frustrating terrorist incidents in 1985, the Reagan administration, determined to take a strong public stand against state-supported terrorism, initiated an intensive coercive strategy against Gaddafi. Although the Reagan administration considered Iran and Syria probably to be greater supporters of terrorism, Libya was a more attractive target for strong coercion because it appeared much more vulnerable to political, economic, and military pressure. In addition, strong circumstantial evidence linked Libya to the December 27, 1985, terrorist attacks in the Rome and Vienna airports, which were the immediate catalysts for the administration's decision to make a powerful, overt response to state-supported terrorism.

The try-and-see variant of coercive diplomacy was employed rather than an ultimatum for several reasons. An ultimatum sets out a short time limit for compliance with one's demand, but the nature of terrorist activity is such that compliance with the demand that it cease is not easily observed and verified. Of course, if immediate noncompliance were the response to the ultimatum, one could soon tell that it had failed. However, much more time would be needed to ascertain compliance with the ultimatum, that is, whether there was indeed a reduction of terrorist attacks encouraged and supported by Gaddafi.

A slowly developing try-and-see approach to coercion recommended itself for other reasons as well. Not all American citizens had as yet left Libya despite the Reagan administration's request several years earlier that they do so. The administration feared that stronger coercive measures against Libya before the remaining U.S. citizens could leave, which they were now sternly enjoined under threat of legal penalty to do, could result in additional hostage-taking. Equally important, the military assets deemed necessary by the Defense Department for any military action were not in place yet. And finally, an incremental approach allowed the administration at least to appeal to its European allies for cooperation in imposing political and economic sanctions against Libya. Such an appeal was consistent with the president's inclination to use military force only as a last resort. Not many in the administration expected much would come of any appeal, but at least it would have been made.

The administration hoped that the tacit threat to escalate to military options against Libya would motivate its allies, reluctant to see force applied, to participate in nonmilitary sanctions. However, Washington did not succeed in developing allied support and meaningful participation in the initial policy of economic and political sanctions against Libya. In the second phase of the try-and-see effort, beginning late in January 1986 the Reagan administration resorted to a show

of military force to impress Gaddafi. Naval and air operations off the coast of Libya were undertaken beginning late
in January and were publicly described as demonstrating
U.S. determination to continue to exercise its rights to operate in international waters and airspace. The administration
had conducted such operations off Libya a number of times
over the course of its tenure. However, sources within the
administration made it clear that the exercises were no coin-
cidence and were "part of the war of nerves." As such, they
were intended to demonstrate, to both Gaddafi and Euro-
peans, that the United States was losing patience with state-
sponsored terrorism and was prepared to take forceful action, if necessary.

Air and naval exercises were repeated in February and
early March, but did not succeed in drawing European allies
into greater cooperation in nonmilitary sanctions against
Libya. And, instead of being intimidated, Gaddafi engaged
in coercive threats of his own. Faced with the failure of its
efforts to impress either its European allies or Gaddafi, the
administration decided in mid-March to step up its try-and-
see approach significantly. U.S. naval forces were now ordered to cross what Gaddafi had earlier labeled the "line of
death" into the Gulf of Sidra in the expectation that this
would provoke a military clash with Libyan military forces,
as it had in 1981. This in fact did occur within a few days
when the Libyan military fired surface-to-air missiles at
American planes. In retaliation, U.S. naval planes attacked a
Libyan air defense missile installation and sank several patrol
boats. It was hoped that this use of force not only would
place additional pressure on Gaddafi to desist from support
of terrorism but also that it might contribute to destabiliza-
tion of his regime and encourage a military coup against
him.

Gaddafi responded by increasing his encouragement of
terrorist activities aimed at Americans. On April 5 a disco-
theque in West Berlin was bombed, killing three persons (two

of them American) and injuring more than two hundred. Complicity in the terrorist bombing was traced to Libya, and the administration now decided upon a major incremental step-up in its coercive strategy. A decision was made to conduct air strikes against five terrorism-related targets in Tripoli and Benghazi (including Gaddafi's command post, where it was supposed he might be). Meanwhile, Washington hoped to avoid allowing its forthcoming action to be portrayed as a strictly U.S.-Libyan confrontation and attempted to gain prior support for the military action from London, Bonn, Paris, and Rome. Only London provided support, allowing U.S. Air Force planes that would be engaged in the operation to use British air bases. U.S Air Force and Navy planes carried out the attack on April 15, inflicting considerable damage on Libyan installations and property, including Gaddafi's headquarters, where a member of his family was killed. This action constituted an "exemplary" use of force because it was coupled with a clear threat to do more to dissuade Gaddafi from continued support of terrorism.

Thus, an incremental progression in coercive measures took place over several months in an effort to make the try-and-see variant of the strategy more effective. Washington had failed in its effort to use the threat of taking military action, something its European allies did not favor, to induce them to participate in meaningful nonmilitary sanctions. Washington had also been unable to create the semblance of a coalition to coerce Gaddafi into stopping his direct support of terrorism. Thereupon, and despite the absence of support from most of its European allies, the administration decided that it must finally back its demands on Gaddafi with major military action.

What, then, was the impact of this coercive military action on Gaddafi's policy of support for international terrorism? As noted earlier, it would take time to make such a determination. In addition, the task of tracing incidents to Gaddafi's

instigation and support would become somewhat more difficult because, it would appear, he took additional steps to hide
involvement in such activities. Nonetheless, evidence of his
continued support for terrorism was documented in the
State Department's annual report, *Patterns of Global Terrorism.*
Gaddafi immediately responded to the April 15 air attacks
with a number of terrorist attacks on U.S. and British personnel. However, in the months following, the State Department was able to report that detectable Libyan involvement
in terrorist activity declined significantly, although it did not
by any means cease. Following a hiatus of a few months, Libyan involvement with terrorism again become apparent. This
activity, some of it conspicuously taking place in 1987 and
1988 on the anniversary of the April 1986 bombing, continued through the close of the Reagan administration. Libya
has never been struck from the State Department's list of
states that support terrorism.

It seems reasonable to conclude on the basis of available
evidence that Colonel Gaddafi did moderate somewhat the
level of his activity and that the April 1986 air attack was a
factor in inducing greater caution and moderation on his
part. However, it is difficult to pin down how important the
administration's coercive policy was in this respect, as other
developments also may have contributed to the apparent reduction of Libyan-supported incidents. As already noted,
Gaddafi made a greater effort to hide his involvement, a factor acknowledged in the State Department reports. Another
development that may have contributed to the apparent reduction in state-sponsored terrorism was the strengthening
of counterterrorism operations by Western governments following the April 1986 bombing attack. In fact these improve-
ments occurred in part as an indirect result of that action.
American's European allies were galvanized to increase their
efforts to combat international terrorism if for no other reason than to reduce the likelihood that the United States

would undertake additional military action. In terms of combating terrorism, increased counterterrorism cooperation was probably the most significant result of the bombing.

Gaddafi was possibly influenced by other political developments into moderating his activities—a military setback in Chad late in 1986 and 1987, Yasser Arafat's renunciation of terrorism in 1989, and dissension within the organization of a leading terrorist, Abu Nidal.

Given the fact that Gaddafi's support for international terrorism did not cease, as the United States had demanded, the question arises whether Washington seriously considered resorting to additional military actions against Libya. At its inception the administration's coercive campaign was to be an open-ended policy of readiness to apply additional military pressure if necessary. In his January 7, 1986, statement announcing the implementation of further economic sanctions against Libya, Reagan had declared, "If these steps do not end Gaddafi's terrorism, I promise you that further steps will be taken." And in his statement following the bombing of Libya, Reagan asserted, "If necessary, we shall do it again." Whatever the administration's intentions in this respect at the outset, however, it is clear that no additional punitive attacks were mounted and it is not certain whether another reprisal raid was seriously considered. There were probably several reasons for this. Military reprisal is not an instrument that presidents can wield easily or frequently. Despite a sense within the administration that the American public would support more military action against Libya, the requirement of indisputable evidence of Gaddafi's complicity in terrorists acts was not easily satisfied. Moreover, perhaps the onset of the Iran-Contra affair in the fall of 1986 distracted the administration and placed it on the political defensive.

7. The Persian Gulf Crisis
A Tough Case for Coercive Diplomacy

This account of the Persian Gulf crisis focuses on the effort to employ coercive diplomacy to induce Saddam Hussein to withdraw from Kuwait and to meet other demands of the UN Security Council. The interpretation is necessarily provisional, as it is based almost entirely on open sources. Two conditions that generally favor the success of coercive diplomacy—strong international and domestic support and a sense of urgency for the opponent's compliance with the demand—were present in this case. Other conditions, however, were not. It is doubtful that Saddam judged the motivation of the U.S.-led coalition to be stronger than his own; in fact, he hoped to split the coalition opposing him. While the United States and its partners were confident that their threat to go to war constituted a powerful and highly credible threat of punishment for noncompliance that should have induced Saddam to back down, the Iraqi leader downgraded the potency of the threatened damage. This was one of Saddam's many miscalculations that contributed to the failure of coercive diplomacy. Finally, the two sides perceived their conflict in zero-sum terms, a psychological perspective that made it extremely difficult for either side to be willing to make the kinds of concessions that could have led to a mutually acceptable compromise.

* * *

To induce Hussein to get out of Kuwait, the UN Security Council employed the strategy of coercive diplomacy. At first, the U.S.-led coalition backed its demand that Iraqi forces get out of Kuwait by imposing economic sanctions and by progressively tightening the embargo on Iraq's imports and exports. This is an example of the variant of coercive diplomacy that has been labelled a gradual turning of the screw. The threat of resorting to military force remained in the background. It was understood from the beginning that economic sanctions, even though unusually tight in this case, would require considerable time to achieve maximum effectiveness and that it was uncertain whether and when they might induce Hussein to comply with the UN demands. Whether the embargo, if given more time, might have succeeded became a controversial, divisive issue in the United States after the administration moved in November to secure a new Security Council resolution authorizing the use of military force at some point after January 15 and began to sound out Congress on the possibility of a similar congressional resolution. Washington also announced in November that an additional 200,000 soldiers would be sent to the Gulf to create an offensive option.

This development marked a significant shift in coercive diplomacy from a gradual turning of the screw via sanctions to an ultimatum backed by the threat of force. There were several reasons for this move to the stronger form of coercive diplomacy, among them the administration's fear that the international coalition might not hold together over the long period required for the embargo to have its full effect. Just as important, if not more so, were personality assessments of Hussein that had come to dominate the administration's thinking. According to psychological profiles of Hussein that circulated in Washington early in the crisis, he was capable of retreat and could indeed be coerced into getting out of Kuwait, but *only* if he were taken to the very brink of war and deprived of any alternative except the stark choice of backing down or being subjected to a devastating all-out war. Leading members of the administration evidently subscribed to this image of Hussein, and they appear to have been rather confident at first that Hussein would back down when the deployment was completed and the coalition's forces in the Gulf reached the stage of full combat readiness sometime in February.

The type of coercive strategy the administration attempted to use against Saddam was a diplomatic version of the well-known game of chicken. The United States deliberately set itself on a collision course with Hussein and tried to convince him that it had thrown away its steering wheel; therefore, a "crash" (that is, war) could be avoided only if he got off the road. To this end the administration repeatedly emphasized that it was embarked on an irreversible course, that the large offensive force being created in the Gulf could not be sustained for a long period and would have to be used sometime before the Muslim holiday of Ramadan in mid-March and certainly before the onset of the hot summer weather in the Gulf. Coupled with this scenario, the Bush administration insisted that there would be no negotiations, no weakening of the UN demands, and no "rewards for aggression."

It would appear, however, that the administration ignored the fact that *both* sides can play the game of diplomatic chicken. As the January 15 deadline set by the Security Council resolution approached, the administration showed signs of increasing perplexity and frustration at indications that Hussein would not back down and instead seemed bent on calling its bluff. The administration also became aware that Hussein had options—for example, beginning a partial withdrawal from Kuwait—and that, if he chose to exercise such options either before or just after January 15, he might well succeed in eroding the coercive pressure of the ultimatum and push the crisis into prolonged negotiations. Although earlier the administration had indicated it would not be in a hurry to initiate war after the January 15 deadline, President Bush eventually decided to do so as soon as possible after January 15 because he was concerned that Saddam might at any moment announce a partial withdrawal from Kuwait or try in other ways to trap the allied coalition into negotiations. Some members of the press referred to this as the administration's "nightmare scenario."

Thus, coercive diplomacy was tried and it failed. The question is why it failed, and what lessons scholars are likely to draw from this case regarding the uses and limitations of the strategy of coercive diplomacy. As was noted in Part One, the strategy of coercive diplomacy is attractive because it offers the possibility of achieving one's objectives without war. But coercive diplomacy assumes a type of simple, uncomplicated rationality on the part of the opponent. The assumption on which coercive diplomacy is based is that if the opponent is rational, he will surely see that it is in his interest to back down. This assumption oversimplifies the roots of motivation and the considerations that may influence leaders who are the targets of coercive diplomacy. The assumption of rationality does not suffice to make a confident prediction as to what an opponent will do when subjected, as Hussein was, to an ultimatum. In this situation, one does not have to be irrational to refuse to knuckle under in the face of the threat of war. The assumption of rationality on which the strategy of coercive diplomacy relies must somehow take into account psychological, cultural, and political variables that can affect the opponent's response to an ultimatum.

One would like to believe that the fateful question of war or peace is not determined by psychological variables having to do with the personalities of leaders. And yet there is reason to believe that in this crisis as well as in the Cuban missile crisis and others, each leader's image of the other and each leader's image of himself do at times play a critically important role in the path to war or peace.

In the case of Hussein, one of the influential psychological profiles of the Iraqi leader referred to earlier that indicated he was capable of retreat also emphasized that *he had to be given a way out that ensured his survival in power.* Otherwise, he would "stop at nothing" and would "use every weapon at his disposal" if he thought his survival in power was at stake.[5]

Future historians are likely to ask whether, instead of going to war with Iraq, it would have been preferable to have given Hussein a better way out than the administration did. The type of coercive diplomacy the Bush administration employed relied almost exclusively on the stick. Whereas Kennedy seriously negotiated with Khrushchev to reach a compromise solution to the missile crisis, the Bush administration rejected any negotiation with Saddam and any compromise settlement. Washington was not willing to go further than to give assurance that it would not attack Iraq if Hussein got out of Kuwait. On occasion administration officials referred to this assurance as a "carrot." But, although in this sense a door was left open for Hussein to escape, the Bush administration made it clear that there could be no "reward for aggression." It rejected any direct linkage of Hussein's withdrawal with a Middle East security conference or with a settlement of the dispute between Iraq and Kuwait that had triggered the war early in August. Nonetheless, had Hussein been willing to take the exit permitted him, he could have avoided the war that followed and survived. We must consider, therefore, why Hussein rejected this opportunity.

It is difficult to avoid the conclusion that in this case the strategy of coercive diplomacy was stretched to its limits and that it is not surprising that it could not produce a peaceful settlement of the crisis. When conflict is viewed in stark zero-sum terms—a perception that both Bush and Hussein appeared to have had—then there is little interest on either side for a mutually acceptable compromise solution. In contrast, Kennedy and Khrushchev did not see their disagreement over the missiles in Cuba as a zero-sum conflict. Rather, they believed that both the United States and the Soviet Union shared an interest in avoiding war and they acted accordingly.

The zero-sum view of the conflict shared by Bush and Hussein, reinforced by the highly invidious image each had of the other, made each leader believe that war would be preferable to the concessions that he would have to make to secure a peaceful settlement. Moreover, each leader held an image of the costs, outcome, and consequences of war that was not distasteful enough to motivate him to seek a compromise settlement. President Bush could view the possibility of war, if his effort at coercive diplomacy failed, with a certain equanimity. War could be accepted as necessary and just in order to punish a ruthless and evil aggressor, deter would-be aggressors in the future, and contribute to the development of a "new world order." In addition, if it came to war, there would then be an opportunity to destroy Iraq's weapons of mass destruction, sharply reduce its overall military capabilities, and thereby eliminate the basis of Hussein's ability to pursue hegemonic aspirations in the region and perhaps even get rid of Hussein himself—objectives the United States could not embrace openly because they would approximate those of a preventive war, which the Security Council had not authorized.

Moreover, the president was reasonably confident that the overwhelming military power of the coalition forces would secure victory with minimal casualties and erase for the American people the bad memory of the Vietnam War. All these considerations combined to reinforce powerfully the president's determination to back Hussein into a corner and to subject him to a humiliating defeat. When war became necessary to accomplish the objective, Bush did not shy away from it.

As for Hussein, he could more easily reject the January 15 ultimatum and call Bush's bluff because he believed that the United States could not tolerate heavy casualties and that his ground forces would be able to inflict them. Besides, if need be, Hussein was not averse to accepting heavy casualties and significant damage from air attacks to Iraq's military infrastructure and civil society. All this would be preferable to giving up the gains of his aggression. Finally, Hussein's motivation and judgment—and his many miscalculations—were influenced by an inflated image of himself as a hero with a mission to transform the Arab world.

Under these circumstances, there was little or no possibility that coercive diplomacy could bring about a mutually acceptable peaceful resolution of the crisis. Later these same considerations defeated the last-minute Soviet effort to arrange a compromise settlement of the war before the U.S.-led coalition launched the powerful ground offensive that inflicted a catastrophic defeat on the Iraqi army. Finally, if the strategy of coercive diplomacy had little chance of success in this case, nonetheless the attempt to employ it in the hope of avoiding war was necessary to build and maintain international and domestic support for the objective of liberating Kuwait; and, ironically, the failure of coercive diplomacy was probably necessary to gain support when war became necessary as "the last resort."

part three

Findings and Conclusions

Analysis of the seven cases presented in Part Two enables us to formulate useful generic knowledge about strategies of coercive diplomacy to supplement the general, abstract model described in Part One. Case studies enable us to understand better the task policymakers face in trying to adapt the general model to a particular situation. The reader will have noted that each of the seven situations described in the case studies had distinctive characteristics. The complex configuration of each case had to be diagnosed by policymakers in order to judge whether a strategy of coercive diplomacy could be designed and implemented well enough to achieve useful results.

Flexibility of the Strategy of Coercive Diplomacy
The case studies provide a vivid demonstration that coercive diplomacy is in fact a very flexible strategy; it can take the form of an ultimatum, a tacit ultimatum, a gradual turning of the screw, or a try-and-see approach. The cases also indicate that which of these variants the policymaker selects is often constrained by characteristics of the particular situation. At the same time, as several of the cases indicate, in

response to crisis developments policymakers may shift from a weaker to a stronger variant of the strategy. Each variant has its own advantages and disadvantages that must be taken into account. (See below for a discussion of the risks of the ultimatum version of the strategy.)

There is another important dimension to the flexibility of coercive diplomacy. Whichever of the four variants of the strategy is chosen, the policymaker does not need to rely solely on coercive threats to induce the opponent to accept what is demanded of him. As in several of the cases, threats may be accompanied by offers of concessions or side-payments—the familiar carrot and stick—that increase the likelihood that the demands will be accepted. What the stick may not be able to accomplish by itself, the addition of a carrot may make it possible for the opponent to accept.

Because coercive diplomacy is a form of crisis bargaining, it is important to recognize that there are three possible components in bargaining: a bargaining strategy can employ coercive threats, accommodative offers, and persuasion. The contribution that persuasion can make to crisis bargaining is often underestimated both in theory and practice. Since by definition coercive diplomacy is a defensive strategy undertaken in response to an opponent's encroachment or aggressive action, the defender often enjoys an inherent advantage insofar as his demand enjoys the kind of legitimacy that norms of international law bestow on the defender. If the defender limits the demands included in his strategy of coercive diplomacy to purely defensive objectives that can be plausibly supported by international norms, then the strategy acquires legitimacy. This legitimacy can be extremely helpful in obtaining international as well as domestic support and in denying the opponent the benefit of international backing. The ability to invoke legitimacy on behalf of one's demands in coercive diplomacy can also be helpful (as in the Cuban missile crisis) in persuading the opponent that his behavior is indefensible and must be altered.

Contextual Variables Affecting Coercive Diplomacy

Another major finding of the study is that coercive diplomacy is highly *context-dependent.* Many different variables can affect the variant of the strategy the policymaker selects, its implementation, and its outcome. These contextual factors vary from one case to another so that one must be careful not to assume that because the strategy worked in one case it ought to be successful in other cases as well. The impact of many different contextual variables means that coercive diplomacy must be tailored in a rather exacting fashion to fit each new situation. Each of the seven cases examined in Part Two offered a fresh challenge to the ability of policymakers to adapt the abstract model of coercive diplomacy to the case at hand.

What are some of these contextual variables? At least eight can be readily identified, some of which were referred to in one or another of the seven case histories.

1. Type of provocation

Crises in which coercive diplomacy is attempted vary greatly in the challenge they pose, depending on the type of provocation that triggered the confrontation. Some types of provocation are easier for the perpetrator to stop or undo, if coerced by the defender, than others. A successful *fait accompli* action that quickly overruns and occupies a neighboring country (as in the case of Iraq's seizure of Kuwait) is more difficult to reverse than an effort to alter a status quo situation by means of a carefully limited probe.

2. Magnitude and depth of the conflict of interests

This factor varies greatly in different crises. To the extent that both sides believe that the crisis engages very important or vital interests, the contest takes on the character of a zero-sum conflict in which one either wins or loses. It is then all the more difficult for coercive diplomacy to achieve a peaceful resolution of the crisis because (as in the Persian Gulf case

in contrast to the Cuban missile case) neither side is willing
to make the concessions needed for a compromise settlement.

3. Image of war
The more horrible the image of war the crisis triggers, the
more strongly motivated one or both sides will be (as in the
Cuban missile crisis but not in the Persian Gulf case) to operate with restraint and to cooperate to avoid such a war.

4. Time pressure to achieve objective
The decision to undertake coercive diplomacy and the pressure to resort to an ultimatum can be influenced by the urgency one feels to resolve the issue. Time urgency can be
experienced for a variety of reasons—for example, concern
that international or domestic support for the policy may de-
cline; awareness that changes in weather will make military
measures more difficult; fear that one's ability to manage the
crisis is breaking down and that one must try to bring it to a
close quickly before it leads to war; concern that the opponent will grow militarily stronger with the passage of time.

5. Unilateral or coalitional coercive diplomacy
Coercive diplomacy is likely to be more difficult when it is
employed by a coalition of states than by a single actor. Although a coalition brings international pressure and perhaps
greater resources to bear on the target of diplomacy, the
unity and sense of purpose of a coalition may be fragile. A
partial exception was the strength and stability of the UN
coalition President Bush succeeded in building on behalf of
coercive diplomacy against Iraq. However, it should be noted
that concern over the vulnerability and lack of staying power
of this coalition was among the considerations that led President Bush to substitute the threat of war for economic sanctions as the main coercive lever in the coalition's strategy.

6. Strong leadership

The choice, implementation, and outcome of coercive diplomacy may depend on the presence of strong and effective top-level political leadership. Such leadership was provided by President Kennedy in the Cuban missile crisis, a factor that undoubtedly contributed to the success of the strategy in that case. In the Persian Gulf crisis, although coercive diplomacy did not succeed and war followed, President Bush's leadership made it possible to create coalition support for the ultimatum to Saddam and for the war that followed when the Iraqi leader refused to accept the demands made on him.

7. The isolation of the adversary

The task of coercive diplomacy is likely to be more complex and difficult when the adversary (as in the Laos crisis of 1961–62 and in the Vietnam 1965 case) is not an isolated state but is supported diplomatically and militarily by allies. Conversely, the virtual diplomatic isolation of Iraq in the recent Gulf crisis and, in particular, the fact that it no longer had the support of the Soviet Union, made it easier for the United States to intervene and to organize the coalition that demanded that Iraq get out of Kuwait.

8. The preferred post-crisis relationship with the adversary

Both the objective of coercive diplomacy and the means employed on its behalf are likely to be sensitive to the type of relationship the coercing power hopes to have with the opponent after the crisis is over. Both Kennedy and Khrushchev hoped to move toward an improvement in U.S.-Soviet relations after reaching a mutually acceptable way of resolving the missile crisis. The contrast with the way the U.S.-led coalition viewed the post-crisis relationship with Saddam Hussein's regime could not be more pronounced.

* * *

The major conclusion we draw from this study is that the strategy of coercive diplomacy is likely to be successful only under certain conditions. This finding is not at all surprising and did not require a study of this kind. What our study adds is an identification of generic problems likely to arise in trying to use the strategy and of various conditions that, if present in a particular case, appear to favor the success of the strategy or, if missing, make failure more likely. Before discussing these conditions we will indicate why it is not always possible or desirable for policymakers to employ the strongest variants of coercive diplomacy—the ultimatum or the tacit ultimatum.

The Constraints and Risks of Ultimatums

Policymakers may consider it necessary to forgo resorting to an ultimatum in situations in which strong domestic or international opposition to such a course of action could result in a severe political-diplomatic backlash. In other situations policymakers may be reluctant to confront the adversary with an ultimatum for fear that it would provoke him to take preemptive military action that would plunge them into a war. In still other situations, policymakers may be uncertain whether the adversary would regard an ultimatum as credible and hence decide to call their bluff, thereby forcing them to choose between initiating military action or backing away from their ultimatum. Another possibility is that the adversary would respond to an ultimatum by indicating conditional or equivocal acceptance of it in a way that would undermine the urgency for compliance with the demands and create strong domestic and international pressures for negotiations aimed at finding a peaceful resolution of the dispute.

For various reasons, therefore, resorting to an ultimatum to enhance the impact of coercive diplomacy may not be desirable or feasible. We have seen how the equivalent of an ultimatum boomeranged in 1941 and provoked the Japanese government into initiating war against the United States. In the Vietnam case, our analysis strongly suggests that President Johnson felt himself severely constrained from coupling air attacks against North Vietnam with a strong variant of coercive diplomacy by lack of domestic political support for American military intervention and by a concern over the risk of provoking escalation. In the Nicaragua case, the Reagan administration's ability to engage in stronger coercive diplomacy against the Sandinista regime was severely constrained by domestic political opposition as well as by strong international opposition. In the Libya case, the ultimatum variant of coercive diplomacy was not employed because it was ill-adapted to the nature of the terrorist activity that the administration was trying to discourage. In the Persian Gulf crisis, the reference to January 15 in the Security Council's resolution authorizing the use of force, if necessary, was not originally intended as a strict deadline for compliance. As events unfolded, however, January 15 came to be viewed as a time-urgent deadline, and military action against Iraq was undertaken soon thereafter.

Components of Crisis Bargaining: Persuasion, Coercion, Accommodation

The two cases in which some version of an ultimatum proved to be effective—the Laos crisis of 1961–62 and the Cuban missile crisis—bear close examination lest an incorrect lesson be drawn that resort to the strong variant of coercive diplomacy was the sole or primary factor contributing to its success in these two cases. Coercive diplomacy is a form of crisis bargaining, and it is instructive to view Kennedy's behavior in these two crises from this standpoint. Crisis bargaining can use persuasion, coercion, and/or accommodation. In any crisis the policymaker must decide *what combination* of these three elements to employ *and in what sequence.*

It is noteworthy that Kennedy employed all three components of crisis bargaining in both the Laos and Cuban crises.

However, the mixture of the three and the sequence in which he brought them into play differed in the two crises. The coercive component of the strategy was significantly greater in the missile crisis, but one should not overlook the fact that his coercive threats were initially coupled with considerable emphasis on persuasion and, toward the end of the crisis, with accommodation. Kennedy believed it was essential to employ coercive threats and actions at the outset of the crisis to demonstrate his resolution and to gain credibility for his warning that he would resort to force if necessary. He gave priority to this objective, deliberately deferring any discussion of concessions until he had first impressed Khrushchev with his resolution. In the Laos crisis, on the other hand, Kennedy began with an emphasis on the possibility of accommodation, signaling a readiness to reduce the American objective in Laos in return for its neutralization. Later, he resorted occasionally to threats of intervention in order to discourage the adversary from exploiting his battlefield advantage too far. The president's threats of intervention were also intended to motivate the Soviet Union to put pressure on its communist allies to operate with restraint and to be more receptive to Kennedy's demands.

In both crises Kennedy began cautiously with the try-and-see variant of coercive diplomacy and shifted to a tacit ultimatum only later when highly disturbing developments made it necessary to do so; and because this fact was evident to his adversary it lent greater credibility and coercive impact to his threat.

It should be noted that Kennedy made considerable use of persuasion in both crises. He employed a variety of diplomatic and open channels to clarify, explain, and justify to his adversary as well as to others why the demand he was making was truly important to the United States and why he was strongly resolved to achieve it. And, cognizant of the principles of crisis management, Kennedy deliberately slowed down the momentum of events, particularly during the Cuban missile crisis, in order to give diplomatic processes and communication an opportunity to work toward a peaceful resolution.

Coercive diplomacy could work in these two cases because neither Kennedy nor Khrushchev viewed the particular conflict of interests in the dispute or their overall relationship as approximating a zero-sum conflict. The objectives Kennedy pursued in both crises, even in the missile crisis, were limited ones. They did not threaten vital Soviet interests. And, as we noted, Kennedy offered substantial carrots as well as making threats in order to secure compliance with his demands. When the conflict with an adversary is viewed in zero-sum terms—as in the case of U.S. policy toward Japan in 1941 and the Bush administration's view of Saddam Hussein in the Gulf crisis—it is much more difficult to employ the carrot-and-stick variant. In extreme cases of this kind, the strategy of coercive diplomacy tends to become all stick and no carrot, and little scope is left for diplomatic efforts to reach a mutually acceptable peaceful resolution of the crisis. Even in these circumstances, however, war is not always inevitable, but a peaceful outcome can then be achieved only if the opponent meets the terms of the ultimatum.

Conditions That Favor Coercive Diplomacy

Because coercive diplomacy is not always successful, it is important to identify conditions that, if present, favor its success or, if absent, reduce the likelihood of its being effective. We use the term "favor" advisedly here because our analysis of historical experience suggests that no single condition can be regarded as a sufficient condition for the success of the strategy. In fact, many variables can have some influence over the outcome of efforts to employ coercive diplomacy. Some of these variables have to do with the content of the particular version of the strategy that is employed—i.e., what is demanded, whether a sense of urgency is created for compliance, whether a threat of punishment for noncompliance is conveyed that is sufficiently credible and potent to overcome the adversary's reluctance to comply with the demands, and whether the threat is coupled with positive incentives and assurances that make it easier for the adversary to accept the demands. Other relevant variables have to do with situational and contextual aspects that were illustrated in the case studies and discussed earlier in this section.

It would be a dangerous oversimplification to believe that coercive diplomacy can always be successful if only one or another condition is satisfied. Thus, for example, we have already noted that it is by no means the case that an ultimatum will always be successful or even that it will always be appropriate. Let us now briefly discuss some of the conditions that favor (although they do not guarantee) effective coercive diplomacy.

1. Clarity of the objective
Although perhaps not always essential, clarity as to the objective of coercive diplomacy—and clarity and consistency in what is demanded of the adversary—is certainly a relevant variable. In both the Laos and Cuban missile crises, this condition was satisfied and contributed to the success of coercive diplomacy. This condition was also present in the Pearl Harbor and Persian Gulf cases, but coercive diplomacy failed for other reasons. In the Vietnam and Nicaragua cases, Washington's objectives and demands were not clear and consistent, and this probably contributed to the difficulties coercive diplomacy encountered in those cases.

Finally, such is the complexity and flexibility of coercive diplomacy, there may be situations in which it is advantageous not to make one's demands too specific or too precise. One such situation arises when the policymaker can be flexible as to how much of a change in the adversary's behavior will suffice.

2. Strength of motivation
Obviously the coercing power must be sufficiently motivated by what it perceives to be at stake in a crisis to act at all, and

sufficient motivation to do so was present in all seven of the cases examined. And yet, as we have seen, coercive diplomacy did not succeed in all of these cases. We conclude, therefore, that while strong motivation is a necessary condition for the success of the strategy, it is clearly not a sufficient condition. Besides, as the next condition highlights, motivation is a two-sided matter.

3. Asymmetry of motivation
The theoretical discussion in Part One and the case studies have stressed the important role that the relative motivation of the two sides plays in determining the outcome of coercive diplomacy. Motivation is fundamentally a function of the interests and values perceived to be at stake and the level of costs and risks one is prepared to accept in protecting them. There are limits on the extent to which real interests can be deliberately exaggerated in order to impress the opponent.

Coercive diplomacy is more likely to be successful if the side employing it is more highly motivated by what is at stake in the crisis than its opponent. What is critical in this respect, however, is that the adversary believe that the coercing power is more highly motivated to achieve its crisis objective than the adversary is to prevent it.

In some cases the relative motivation of the two sides tends to be fixed by the nature of the conflict. In other cases, however, the side that engages in coercive diplomacy may be able to create an asymmetry of motivation in its favor in two ways: by demanding of the opponent only what is essential to protect its own vital interests and by not making demands that engage the vital interests of its adversary; or by offering a carrot that reduces the adversary's motivation to resist the demands. In the Laos and Cuban missile crises, as we have seen, Kennedy used both of these levers to create an asymmetry of motivation in his favor. The success of his coercive threats in these two cases cannot be properly understood without taking this leverage into account. In contrast, the

United States was not able to create in its opponent a perception that an asymmetry of motivation operated in favor of
the United States in the Pearl Harbor, Vietnam, Nicaragua,
and Persian Gulf cases. In these four cases, the U.S. demands
engaged what the opponent perceived as vital interests and
strengthened the opponent's motivation not to comply. And
in all four cases, insignificant carrots, or none at all, were
offered. We regard the absence of asymmetry as an important part of the explanation for the failure of coercive diplomacy in these cases.

4. Sense of urgency
It is, once again, the opponent's perception of the condition
that is critical. Of course, if the state employing coercive diplomacy genuinely experiences a sense of urgency to achieve
its objective—as Kennedy did in the Cuban case—it is more
likely to be able to generate a sense of urgency for compliance on the part of the opponent. Otherwise, the coercing
power must find other ways of conveying a credible sense of
urgency for compliance. The presence of this condition in
the Laos and Cuban missile crises contributed importantly to
the success of coercive diplomacy in those two cases. On the
other hand, as the Pearl Harbor case instructs us, creating a
sense of urgency for compliance with one's demand may
boomerang and encourage a desperate opponent to initiate
war in preference to accepting onerous demands. A sense of
urgency for compliance was not effectively communicated in
the Vietnam and Nicaragua cases. In the Persian Gulf crisis
a sense of urgency was created by treating January 15 as a
deadline for compliance but, for the reasons indicated in the
case study, Saddam Hussein preferred war to capitulation.

5. Adequate domestic and international support
A certain level of political support at home is needed for any
serious use of coercive diplomacy by American leaders. It is
difficult to go beyond this simple generalization, however,

because the extent to which the strategy depends on domestic political support can vary substantially depending on the ·specifics of the case, in particular how quickly the crisis is concluded. Inadequate domestic support seems certainly to have constrained the use of coercive diplomacy against Vietnam and Nicaragua. In contrast, there was considerable support for Kennedy's handling of the Cuban missile crisis and Reagan's effort to coerce Gaddafi into giving up support for international terrorism.

International support (or lack thereof) is also an important factor in some cases. The support of the Organization of American States and the United Nations was certainly helpful to Kennedy in the missile crisis. In contrast, concern about international reactions contributed to Johnson's cautious use of air power against North Vietnam, and the opposition of Central American leaders to stronger coercive measures by the United States against Nicaragua motivated them to undertake independent efforts at mediation. On the other hand, limited international support did not prevent the Reagan administration from carrying out the bombing attack against Libya.

Unusually strong international and domestic support in the Persian Gulf crisis made it possible for the Bush administration to adopt an ultimatum strategy; however, the presence of this support did not sufficiently impress Saddam Hussein to lead him to agree to the demands of the UN coalition.

6. Opponent's fear of unacceptable escalation
The impact of coercive diplomacy is enhanced if the initial steps taken against the adversary arouse his fear of escalation to levels of warfare that he would regard as unacceptable and would be strongly motivated to avoid. This happened in both the Laos and Cuban missile crises. In the Libyan case, the U.S. air strike appears to have had a similar intimidating effect for a time. The Pearl Harbor case is different in that the

U.S. oil embargo already constituted an escalation of the crisis that was unacceptable to the Japanese, who then regarded their options as limited either to securing an alleviation of the oil embargo through diplomacy or going to war. In the Vietnam case, there is little evidence that the limited U.S. air attacks of early 1965 created fear on Hanoi's part of unacceptable escalation of the conflict. In the Nicaraguan case, the Sandinista leadership may have been concerned over the possibility of direct U.S. military intervention earlier in the crisis, but this factor clearly did not operate in motivating them to accept the formula for ending the crisis developed by the Central American leaders. In the Persian Gulf crisis, Saddam Hussein apparently underestimated the strength of the military blow the U.S.-led coalition was capable of inflicting, and for this and perhaps other reasons he was not intimidated enough to accept the demands of the Security Council.

7. Clarity concerning the precise terms of settlement of the crisis

Clarity of objectives and demands (the first condition listed above) may not suffice; in addition, it may be necessary in some cases (as, for example, in the Cuban crisis) for the coercing power to formulate rather specific terms regarding the termination of the crisis the two sides have agreed upon and to establish procedures for carrying out these terms and verifying their implementation.

This condition can be of major importance also to the adversary's side. It may desire precise settlement terms to safeguard against the possibility that the coercing power has in mind a broader, more sweeping interpretation of the formula for ending the crisis or will be tempted to renew pressure and push for even greater concessions after the initial agreement for terminating the crisis is concluded. The adversary who has succumbed to coercive diplomacy may need specific and reliable assurances that the coercive power will carry out its part of the termination agreement.

* * *

Not all of these seven conditions appear to be equally important for the success of coercive diplomacy efforts. The three that seem particularly significant for influencing the outcome have to do with *the opponent's perception*. Thus, coercive diplomacy is facilitated if the opponent believes that an asymmetry of motivation operates in favor of the coercing power, that it is really time-urgent to respond to the coercing power's demands, and that the opponent must take seriously the possibility that the coercing power will engage in escalation that would pose unacceptable costs. As all three of these conditions are perceptions held by the leaders of the state that is being subjected to coercive diplomacy, it should be clear that whether this strategy will work in any particular case rests in the last analysis on psychological variables. This fact introduces considerable uncertainty into efforts to ensure the success of coercive diplomacy against a particular opponent.

One need not elaborate upon these uncertainties to note that when subjective, psychological variables play so important a role in determining the outcome of a conflict, the possibility of misperceptions and miscalculations by either side is ever present and can render calculation and prediction of the adversary's behavior hazardous.

Adding to the risks of the strategy is the fact that the policymaker employing coercive diplomacy often cannot reliably judge whether these conditions are sufficiently present or can be created in the case at hand. Further, the informational requirements of the strategy in many cases are complex and difficult to meet. A particularly good knowledge of the opposing leaders, their mind-sets, and the domestic and international contexts in which they are operating is necessary to estimate their motivations and their cost-benefit calculations. And such estimates often have to be made on the basis of fragmentary and equivocal information.

Conclusions

Our analysis of seven attempts to employ coercive diplomacy highlights several important characteristics of the strategy. Coercive diplomacy is a very *flexible* strategy that is highly *context-dependent;* its success depends heavily on *adapting* the abstract model (outlined in Part One) to the specific configuration and dynamics of a particular situation, and on *skill in implementation.*

The general strategy of coercive diplomacy is strikingly flexible in three basic respects. The demand made of the opponent is a variable that significantly influences the prospects for success. The demand may be very modest—as in President Kennedy's effort in the Laos crisis to get the other side to cooperate with his effort to reduce the U.S. commitment to the anticommunist Laotian government and to obtain agreement for neutralization of the whole country. Or, as in the Pearl Harbor and Nicaragua cases, the demand may require the opponent to give up a great deal affecting his vital interests.

The strategy is very flexible also in how much of a carrot, if any, the opponent is offered to induce compliance with the demand. As we have seen, little or no carrot was offered Saddam Hussein in the Gulf crisis, Gaddafi in the Libyan case, or the Sandinistas in the Nicaragua case; and only a modest one was conveyed to the Japanese in the negotiations preceding the attack on Pearl Harbor. In contrast, quite substantial carrots were offered the other side in the Laos and Cuban missile crises.

A third aspect of the flexibility of coercive diplomacy is that it has four significantly different variants: the ultimatum, the tacit ultimatum, the gradual turning of the screw, and the try-and-see approach. These forms of the strategy vary in coercive impact and in their capacity to influence the adversary. The state that chooses to employ coercive diplomacy seldom has an unencumbered choice of which variant of the strategy to employ, as there can be significant constraints on how to proceed. As experience has demonstrated, policymakers may decide not to resort to an ultimatum because they are unwilling to accept the associated risks.

In judging whether coercive diplomacy is likely to be a viable strategy in any particular situation, policymakers will do well to weigh carefully whether the demand on the opponent they plan to make, the coercive threat they can convey, the carrot they may offer, and the resolution they can display are likely together to create the following three beliefs in the adversary's mind: (1) the perception that an asymmetry of interest and motivation exists that favors the coercer; (2) a sense of urgency for compliance with the demand; and (3) a judgment that the threatened punishment is credible and potent enough to overcome his reluctance to comply with the demand. Although our research does not enable us to state that these three perceptual variables are strictly necessary or sufficient conditions for the success of coercive diplomacy, the case studies indicate that the presence of these beliefs in the mind of the target of coercive diplomacy strongly favors the success of the strategy.

All this means that policymakers must tailor the abstract model of coercive diplomacy in a rather exacting manner to fit the special configuration and context of each situation. This is a challenging task, as the relevant characteristics of a situation are not always clearly visible or easily appraised by policymakers. And, as has been noted, many contextual variables influence the workings and outcome of efforts at coercive diplomacy.

Efforts to use coercive diplomacy effectively rest heavily on skill in improvisation. The importance of timing is often crucial. The adversary must be permitted an opportunity to digest the situation as presented and to reflect carefully, even though giving him time to do so may dilute the sense of urgency for compliance. The nation that adopts this strategy assumes responsibility for pacing events, for determining the appropriate sense of urgency to create, and for clear and timely communications. It must weigh carefully how the opponent is responding to developments in considering what to do next. Reliable insight into the mind-set of the opponent is necessary to orchestrate the strategy skillfully; without it the actions taken to influence him can easily backfire, triggering critical misperceptions and miscalculations. Indeed, the state that engages in coercive diplomacy can seldom have full or reliable control over the outcome because so much depends on the adversary's assessment of the situation.

For all these reasons, there will be few crises in which coercive diplomacy will constitute a high-confidence strategy. If it can be made to work, it is indeed a less costly way of achieving one's objectives than exclusive reliance on military force. Coercive diplomacy is a sharp tool—at times useful, but difficult to employ successfully against a recalcitrant or unpredictable opponent. Although the strategy sometimes assumes an attraction that may be difficult to resist, its apparent advantages should not be allowed to distort judgment of its feasibility in any particular situation.

It is hoped that the analysis presented in this monograph of the variants of coercive diplomacy, the constraints that may come into play in designing and implementing the strategy in different situations, and the conditions that influence its effectiveness will help policymakers to judge the uses and limitations of the strategy.

Notes

Preface
1. A. L. George, *Some Thoughts on Graduated Escalation*, RM-4844-PR (Santa Monica, Calif.: The RAND Corporation, 1965).

2. The first published account of these procedures was my chapter, "Case Studies and Theory Development: The Method of Structured, Focused Comparison," in Paul G. Lauren, ed., *Diplomatic History: New Approaches in History, Theory, and Policy* (New York: The Free Press, 1979).

3. Alexander L. George, David K. Hall, and William E. Simons, *The Limits of Coercive Diplomacy* (Boston: Little, Brown and Co., 1971).

Part One
Theory of Coercive Diplomacy
1. I should remind the reader that the definitions offered here (as is true of most definitions of complex phenomena) tend to over-simplify reality and are best regarded as a starting point for empirical analysis of those phenomena that should go beyond the confines of the definition.

2. The concept of "exemplary" use of force presented here as a possible component of coercive diplomacy is not always easily distinguishable in historical situations from the practice of retaliation and reprisal. Strictly speaking, the term "reprisal" should be reserved for an action that is limited in purpose to punishing an opponent in some appropriate way for a transgression. Retaliation and reprisal may also constitute what some writers refer to as "active deterrence." In contrast, the purpose of an exemplary use of force in coercive diplomacy is to convey a willingness to do more, if necessary, to persuade the opponent to stop or undo his transgression. Particularly when the offended state does not make clear whether the action it takes is merely a reprisal or an exemplary component of coercive diplomacy, the historian will have difficulty determining the purpose of that action.

Part Two
Practice of Coercive Diplomacy

   1. This methodology is described in detail in A. L. George, "Case Studies," in Paul G. Lauren, ed., *Diplomatic History*.

   2. As for the United States, variants of coercive diplomacy were also attempted in a number of other crises: for example, in the early phase of its response to the North Korean attack on South Korea in June 1950; in the threat of financial pressure President Eisenhower made to induce England to call off its war against Egypt in 1956; in President Nixon's effort to induce a withdrawal of the Syrian tanks that invaded Jordan in 1970; in President Reagan's effort to deal with Syrian involvement in Lebanon in 1982; and perhaps at an early stage in the Iran hostage crisis of 1979–81. No doubt other cases could be found in which the United States attempted the strategy of coercive diplomacy.

   Of course, other states have also used this strategy. Stalin blockaded Allied ground access to West Berlin in 1948 in order to pressure the Western powers to give up their new policy toward the Western zones of occupied Germany. In the Sino-Soviet border crisis of 1969, Khrushchev finally threatened to destroy China's nuclear facilities to induce Mao to cease his provocations. In the Falkland Islands case, the British use of coercive diplomacy failed to induce a withdrawal of Argentine forces and war followed.

   3. Historical instances in which the United States decided not to employ coercive diplomacy to deal with a hostile action include the Iran crisis of 1946; the Berlin blockade crisis of 1948–49; the Taiwan Strait crisis of 1954–55; the Quemoy crisis of 1958; and the *Pueblo* and *Mayaguez* incidents of 1968 and 1975.

   4. Whether to regard these early air attacks as an example of the "exemplary" use of force cannot be easily decided and must rest on the investigator's judgment, a matter on which scholars may disagree. I am inclined not to regard these actions as an exemplary use of force because I interpret them as part of the weak try-and-see variant of coercive diplomacy. However, because the available data indicate that the administration accompanied the air attacks with at least vague threats of heavier punishment if necessary, it is not implausible to regard them as exemplary in purpose. I am indebted to David Newsom for calling this possibility to my attention.

5. See, for example, Jerrold M. Post, M.D., "Saddam Hussein of Iraq: An Analysis of his Personality and Political Behavior," unpublished manuscript, September 14, 1990. A more detailed version of this paper was presented by Dr. Post in his testimony before the House Armed Services Committee on December 5 and the House Foreign Affairs Committee on December 11, 1990.

Bibliographical Notes and Acknowledgments

Part One of this monograph draws on and updates the discussion of the theory of coercive diplomacy presented in a previous publication, *The Limits of Coercive Diplomacy: Laos, Cuba, Vietnam* by Alexander L. George, David K. Hall, and William E. Simons (Boston: Little, Brown & Co., 1971). Its authors are updating and revising the three case studies reported in that book, and some of the results of their work in progress have been available for the present monograph.

The brief summary of the Pearl Harbor case draws on the detailed research of Scott D. Sagan, part of which he published in "The Origins of the Pacific War," *Journal of Interdisciplinary History* (Spring 1988), pp. 323–352. Sagan's work is based on careful analysis of the rich secondary literature on the origins of the war and pertinent documentary materials. Use has been made also of the brief treatment of the Pearl Harbor case in Gordon A. Craig and Alexander L. George, *Force and Statecraft: Diplomatic Problems of Our Time*, 2nd edition (New York: Oxford University Press, 1990), pp. 203–206.

The account of the Laos crisis of 1961–62 draws on David Hall's analysis of the case in *The Limits of Coercive Diplomacy*, pp. 36–85, and his subsequent treatments of it in "The Laotian War of 1962" in Barry M. Blechman and Stephen S. Kaplan, *Force Without War: U.S. Armed Forces as a Political Instrument* (Washington, D.C.: The Brookings Institution, 1978), pp. 135–174; and "The Laos

Neutralization Agreement, 1962," in Alexander L. George, ed., *U.S.-Soviet Security Cooperation; Achievements, Failures, Lessons* (New York: Oxford University Press, 1988), pp. 435–465. Hall's analysis is based on a thorough evaluation of available archival materials as well as the secondary sources on the crisis.

The summary of the Cuban missile crisis draws on George's earlier analysis of the case (*Limits of Coercive Diplomacy*, pp. 86–143) and his recent update of it, using new materials and recent accounts of the crisis, that appears as a chapter in Alexander L. George, ed., *Avoiding War: Problems of Crisis Management* (Boulder, Colo.: Westview Press, 1991).

The Vietnam case study benefits from the thorough research in archival as well as secondary sources conducted over many years by William E. Simons, who was also the author of two classified monographs on aspects of the Vietnam war that appeared in what came to be known as *The Pentagon Papers*. Simons prepared an unclassified version of the case based on public sources that was published in *Limits of Coercive Diplomacy*, pp. 144–210. He has since updated his earlier work on the basis of a thorough examination of all available archival sources and a study of new scholarly treatments of the case published by other investigators. Simons has kindly made available several of his recent unpublished studies, which have been used in preparing the summary of the case.

A great deal has been written on the efforts of the Reagan administration to employ some version of coercive diplomacy against the Sandinista regime in Nicaragua. Much was written during the course of this long crisis and dealt with contemporary developments. It will take time for well-researched, scholarly accounts to emerge. The brief summary of the case presented here draws largely on Kenneth Roberts' recent analytical account, which employs the framework of coercive diplomacy and draws on the available public record. (See his article, "Bullying and Bargaining: The United States, Nicaragua, and Conflict Resolution in Central America," *International Security*, vol. 15, no. 2 [Fall 1990], pp. 67–102.) The case study presented in this monograph also benefited from Bruce Jentleson's current research on this case and his article, "The Reagan Administration and Coercive Diplomacy: Restraining More Than Remaking Governments," *Political Science Quarterly*, vol. 106, no. 1 (Spring 1991), pp. 57–82.

The brief summary of the Libyan case is drawn largely from an incisive analysis by Tim Zimmerman that views it from the standpoint of the theory of coercive diplomacy: "The American Bombing of Libya: A Success of Coercive Diplomacy?" *Survival*, vol. 29, no. 3 (May/June 1987), pp. 195–214. Mr. Zimmerman kindly made available for this study a more recent evaluation he has prepared of the impact of the air bombing on Gaddafi's policy. Also helpful is the detailed account, based partly on interviews with American policymakers, in David C. Martin and John Walcott, *Best Laid Plans: The Inside Story of America's War Against Terrorism* (New York: Harper and Row, 1988), pp. 67–83, 258–322.

The account of the Persian Gulf crisis is based on newspaper sources. Particularly useful were Don Oberdoerfer's "Missed Signals in the Middle East," *Washington Post*, Sunday, March 19, 1991, and Bob Woodward, *The Commanders* (New York: Simon and Schuster, 1991). The author has benefited from conversations with many individuals, in particular Professor Richard Herrmann, who is preparing a case study of this crisis.

Useful comments on an earlier draft of the manuscript were provided by two reviewers: David Newsom and another who remains confidential. Anne Cushman provided efficient and cheerful secretarial assistance.

Finally, the author wishes to thank the Carnegie Corporation of New York for a grant that facilitated work on this and related research projects.

* * *

A very large body of literature deals with the use of threats of force and limited force as instruments of diplomacy. Only a few of these publications can be listed here.

Barry M. Blechman, Stephen S. Kaplan, et al., *Force Without War: U.S. Armed Forces as a Political Instrument* (Washington, D.C.: The Brookings Institution, 1978).

Gordon A. Craig and Alexander L. George, *Force and Statecraft: Diplomatic Problems of Our Time*, 2nd ed. (New York: Oxford University Press, 1990).

Bradford Dismukes and James McConnell, eds., *Soviet Naval Diplomacy* (New York: Pergamon Press, 1979).

Alexander L. George, ed., *Avoiding War: Problems of Crisis Management* (Boulder, Colo.: Westview Press, 1991).

Gary Hufbauer and Jeffrey Schott, *Economic Sanctions Reconsid-*

ered: History and Current Policy (Washington, D.C.: Institute of International Economics, 1985).

Paul Gordon Lauren, ed., *Diplomacy: New Approaches in History, Theory, and Policy* (New York: Free Press, 1979).

Richard Ned Lebow, *Between Peace and War: The Nature of International Crisis* (Baltimore: Johns Hopkins University Press, 1981).

Thomas C. Schelling, *Arms and Influence* (New Haven, Conn.: Yale University Press, 1966).

Glenn H. Snyder and Paul Diesing, *Conflict Among Nations* (Princeton, N.J.: Princeton University Press, 1977).

Oran R. Young, *The Politics of Force* (Princeton, N.J.: Princeton University Press, 1968).

Index

Accommodation, 68, 73–75
Air strikes
  against Libya, 56, 79
  against North Vietnam, 39–46, 73, 79
Arafat, Yasser, 58
Asymmetry of motivation, 13, 36, 45, 77–78, 81, 83

Bargaining. *See* Crisis bargaining
Blackmail strategy, 5
Bush, George, 48, 62, 63, 64–65, 70, 71

Carrot-and-stick approach, 10–11, 22, 27–28, 35, 46, 47, 49, 63, 68, 75, 77–78, 82
Castro, Fidel, 13, 32
Central America, 48, 51, 79, 80. *See also* Nicaragua
Central Intelligence Agency, 50
Chamorro, Violetta, 48
China, 25, 27, 28–29, 40, 42, 44
Coalitional coercive diplomacy, 70
Coercion, 5–6, 9, 68, 73–75
Coercive diplomacy
  benefits, 6, 84
  central task, 11–14
  coalitional, 70
  components, 7
  conditions favoring, 75–81
  defensive nature, 5, 68
  flexibility of, 5, 67–68, 82
  object of, 21
  theory, 3–14
  unilateral, 70
  variants, 7–9, 67–68, 82–83
Communication levels, 9–10
Compellance, 5
Conflict of interests, 69–70
Context-dependence, 16, 21, 69–72, 82
Contextual variables, 69–72
Contras, 48, 49–50, 51
Crisis bargaining, 33, 34, 36, 68, 73–75
Cuban missile crisis, 11, 13, 31–37, 63, 64, 73–74, 76, 77, 78, 79

Defensive nature of coercive diplomacy, 5, 68
Deterrence, 20–21
Diplomatic chicken, 61–62
Dobrynin, Anatoly, 35
Domestic support, 46, 50, 59, 73, 78–79
Dulles, John Foster, 26

Economic sanctions, 20, 50, 51, 54, 60
Eisenhower, Dwight D., 26
El Salvador, 47
Escalation, fear of, 36–37, 79–80, 81
Exemplary action, 5–6, 29, 56

Gaddafi, Muammar, 53–58, 79, 82
Geneva conference, 43, 45–46
Gradual-turning-of-the-screw approach, 8–9, 50, 60, 67, 82
Great Britain, 56

Hussein, Saddam, 59–60, 61–62, 63, 64, 65, 71, 75, 78, 79, 80, 82

Image of war, 36–37, 70
Inducements. *See* Carrot-and-stick approach
International norms, 68
International support, 40, 46, 50, 56, 59, 70, 73, 78–79
Iran, 53
Iran-Contra scandal, 50, 58
Iraq. *See* Persian Gulf crisis
Isolation of the adversary, 71

Johnson, Lyndon B., 39–46, 73

Kennedy, John F.
  Cuban missile crisis, 11, 13, 31–37, 63, 64, 71, 73–75, 77
  Laos crisis, 6, 25–30, 43, 44, 73–75, 77
Khrushchev, Nikita
  Cuban missile crisis, 13, 31, 32, 33, 34, 35, 36, 37, 63, 64, 71, 74, 75
  Laos crisis, 27, 28–29, 30, 75
Kuwait. *See* Persian Gulf crisis

Laos crisis (1961–62), 6, 25–30, 43, 71, 73, 76, 77, 78, 79, 82
Leadership, 71
Legitimacy, 68

Libyan-inspired terrorism, 53–58, 73, 79
Lippmann, Walter, 46

Misperception and miscalculation, 4, 10, 14, 23, 37, 59, 81, 84
Motivation, 11–14, 36, 45, 76–78, 81, 83
Multinational opponents, 27, 43

Nicaragua, 47–52, 73, 76, 78, 79, 80, 82
Nidal, Abu, 58
Nonverbal communication, 9–10

Objectives, 12–13, 19, 21–22, 25–26, 32, 36, 44, 47–48, 76
Oil embargo of Japan, 19–20, 22, 80
Opponent's perceptions, 12, 14, 37, 59–60, 63, 64–65, 81–82, 83, 84
Organization of American States, 79
Ortega, Daniel, 48

Pathet Lao forces, 25, 26, 27, 28, 29, 30
Patterns of Global Terrorism, 57
Pearl Harbor, 19–23, 72–73, 75, 76, 78, 79–80, 82
Perceptions of opponent, 12, 14, 37, 59–60, 63, 64–65, 81–82, 83, 84
Persian Gulf crisis, 10–11, 59–65, 70, 71, 73, 75, 76, 78, 79, 80
Personalities of leaders, 37, 61, 63, 81–82
Persuasion, 68, 73–75
Post-crisis relationship, 71
Provocation type, 69
Psychological variables, 14, 37, 62, 63, 81–82

Qaddafi, Muammar. *See* Gaddafi, Muammar

Rationality, 4, 37, 62
Reagan, Ronald, 58, 79
Reagan administration, 47, 48, 54–55
Roosevelt, Franklin D., 20, 22
Royal Lao government, 25, 28, 30
Rusk, Dean, 46

Sandinistas, 47–52, 73, 80, 82
Schelling, Thomas, 5
Settlement terms, 80–81
Signaling, 6, 9–10, 33
Southeast Asia Treaty Organization, 26
Soviet Union
    Cuban missile crisis, 13, 32
    Laos crisis, 25, 27, 28–29, 74
    Nicaragua, 50
    Persian Gulf crisis, 65
    Vietnam, 40, 42, 43, 44
Stopping vs. undoing, 6, 69
Syria, 53

Tacit ultimatum, 8, 28, 67, 74, 82
Terrorism, 53–58, 73, 79
Thailand, 26, 28, 29, 30
Threat of punishment, 4, 10, 11–12, 13–14, 19, 29, 50, 83

Time limits, 7–8, 19–20, 28, 35–36, 45, 50, 59, 70, 73, 78, 81, 83, 84
Timing, 83–84
Try-and-see approach, 8, 27, 32, 35, 42, 45, 50–51, 54, 67, 74, 83

U-2 incident, 34–35, 36, 37
Ultimatums, 7, 8, 23, 35–36, 54, 60, 67, 76, 82
    constraints and risks, 23, 72–73
    tacit, 8, 28, 67, 74, 82
Unilateral coercive diplomacy, 70
United Nations, 79
United Nations Security Council, 59, 60, 64, 73, 80
U.S.-Japan relations leading to Pearl Harbor, 19–23, 72–73, 75, 76, 78, 79–80
Urgency, sense of, 7–8, 19–20, 35–36, 45, 50, 59, 70, 73, 78, 81, 83, 84

Vietnam (1965), 39–46, 71, 73, 76, 78, 79

Zero-sum conflict, 45, 60, 64–65, 69–70, 75

Jennings Randolph Program for International Peace

As part of the statute establishing the United States Institute of Peace, Congress envisioned a fellowship program that would appoint "scholars and leaders of peace from the United States and abroad to pursue scholarly inquiry and other appropriate forms of communication on international peace and conflict resolution." The program was named after Senator Jennings Randolph of West Virginia, whose efforts over four decades helped to establish the Institute.

Since it began 1987, the Jennings Randolph Program has played a key role in the Institute's effort to build a national center of research, dialogue, and education on critical problems of conflict and peace. Through a rigorous annual competition, outstanding men and women from diverse nations and fields are selected to carry out projects designed to expand and disseminate knowledge on violent international conflict and the wide range of ways it can be peacefully managed or resolved.

The Institute's Distinguished Fellows and Peace Fellows are individuals from a wide variety of academic and other professional backgrounds who work at the Institute on research and education projects they have proposed and participate in the Institute's collegial and public outreach activities. The Institute's Peace Scholars are doctoral candidates at American universities who are working on their dissertations.

Institute fellows and scholars have worked on such varied subjects as international negotiation, regional security arrangements, conflict resolution techniques, international legal systems, ethnic and religious conflict, arms control, and the protection of human rights. These issues have been examined in settings throughout the world, including the Soviet Union, Europe, Latin America, sub-Saharan Africa, and South Asia.

As part of its effort to disseminate original and useful analyses of peace and conflict to policymakers and the public, the Institute publishes book manuscripts and other written products that result from the fellowship work and meet the Institute's high standards of quality.

Michael S. Lund
Director